The Blue and White Room

The Blue and White Room

by MARY GILLIATT

Foreword by
Pierre Moulin and Pierre LeVec

Design by
Timothy Shaner

BANTAM BOOKS

NEW YORK   TORONTO   LONDON   SYDNEY   AUCKLAND

THE BLUE AND WHITE ROOM

A Bantam Book / November 1992

Grateful acknowledgment is made for permission to reprint from *Collected Poems* by
Wallace Stevens. Copyright 1923 and renewed 1951 by Wallace Stevens.
Reprinted by permission of Alfred A. Knopf, Inc.

Library of Congress Cataloging-in-Publication Data

Gilliatt, Mary
The Blue and White Room / by Mary Gilliatt:
foreword by Pierre Moulin and Pierre LeVec.
p.   cm.
ISBN 0-553-07761-9
1. Blue in interior decoration.   2. White in interior decoration.
3. Decoration and ornament, Rustic–France.   I. Title
NK2115.5.C6G48   1992
747'.94—dc20   92-739

Published simultaneously in the United States and Canada

Bantam Books are published by Bantam Books, a division of Bantam Doubleday
Dell Publishing Group, Inc. Its trademark, consisting of the words "Bantam Books"
and the portrayal of a rooster, is Registered in U.S. Patent and Trademark Office
and in other countries. Marca Registrada. Bantam Books, 666 Fifth
Avenue, New York, New York 10103.

PRINTED IN HONG KONG

0 9 8 7 6 5 4 3 2 1

Dedication

For my first grandchild, Olivia Constantine, who has a
beautiful blue and white room of her own.

Acknowledgments

I particularly want to thank the following people: Coleen O'Shea of
Bantam and my editor and friend Barbara Plumb (who had the idea for
this book in the first place) for all their help, understanding, and input;
Tim Shaner, who designed the book so beautifully; William Nabers, a man
of discernment, who so diligently found pictures; Alexander Theroux,
whose research on the color blue I found so helpful; Mark Collins and
Gabrielle Townsend of Collins and Brown, who were so enthusiastic
about a book on blue and white rooms; and Sue Breger, Barbara Prisco,
and Sandy Dolnier, who have made my life much easier in so many ways.

CONTENTS

Foreword

In the past twenty-five years at Pierre Deux, our forte has been French Country Style, which we have seen evolve and eventually become a classic style of interior design in its own right. We have enjoyed seeing people embrace the casual yet elegant ambience of the style we feel so comfortable with.

When we first began importing the Souleiado fabrics from Provence these cottons were primarily the traditional provençal patterns of bright and busily patterned, multicolored florals with coordinating borders. Because of the large number of patterns in many different colors, we had to be very careful not to create a mishmash or a conflict of colors while designing our shops to showcase this collection. Always adding to the collection, designer David Hicks created a new coordinating group of simple geometrics, completely done in just two colors: Blue and white!

This presented a new challenge. We immediately sensed that this bi-color collection could not be shown mixed up among the others. It had to have its own space, and, as we grew to enjoy this combination more and more, its own room. However, to stand on its own, we discovered that it had to be executed in abundance—walls, windows, bed treatments—"the works." It was like Delft tiling the entire room! The result was a strong and refreshing statement. An oasis of blue and white surrounded by a profusion of color. The whole room looked like a blue sky on a beautiful day filled with white billowing cumulus clouds.

We loved our blue and white room. With its whitewashed floor and beams, it was so fresh and simple, which made accessorizing easy. One day a bowl of green Granny Smiths, the next a pitcher of buttery yellow daffodils. We could literally watch people being drawn by our oasis of heavenly blue and white.

Several years later, we had the opportunity to again feature a room of our favorite duet of colors, when we reintroduced another classic—the collection of authentic Oberkampf Toile de Jouy. My favorite, as well as Pierre's, the blue and white "Le Ballon de Gonesse," shown in the book's introductory essay, The Blue and White Tradition, depicts man's first flight in a

Eighteenth-century limestone trumeau mantel from the Saintonge region of France, with a boarder of Delft tiles.

Foreword

hot air balloon. The historic pattern is perfect for wall upholstery, due to its open and large repeat (39"). No one tires of this classic *bleu et blanc* panoramic view of blue balloons rising above the Champ-de-Mars.

On a buying trip some time ago, in Toulouse at the antique fair, we bought for ourselves a marvelous eighteenth-century trumeau mantel. The mantelpiece, hand-carved in French limestone and bordered in Delft tiles, was irresistible to us, although we had nowhere appropriate to install it due to its large scale. However, we knew we had to have it. As a matter of fact, it sat waiting at our transporters in Paris for two years. Then, out of the blue, we found the perfect country house with a dining room that needed a well-proportioned centerpiece. We finished the dining room in blue and white, by adding a pine armoire filled with our collection of blue and white Chantilly porcelain. Then, to accommodate everyone during the holidays, we mixed two sets of painted chairs of blue and white with rush seats. It is casual yet elegant and, by candlelight, luminous and joyous!

Pure in its simplicity, blue and white as a color scheme has become a classic French Country Interior Design, and a favorite in our homes.

Pierre Moulin
Pierre LeVec

The Blue
and White
Room

The Blue and White Tradition

I love blue and white. So, it appears, does a very large part of the world, judging by the number of different geographical locations represented in the photographs of this book. Blue and white is surely used more often than other popular pairings, such as black and white, red and white, green and white, and yellow and white. So why is blue and white so universally beloved? It is not just for reasons of esthetics—although it is certainly one of the leading factors—for both colors have a wider range of tones than almost any other color, all of which go beautifully together in any permutation. Nor is it the fact that blue pigments were so rare and expensive for so long that the color became especially prized. I think that like a good many instinctive choices we make in decoration (and the choice of color is nothing if not emotive), it is because of various conditionings of which we may hardly be aware. A conditioning formed, first of all, because so much of nature—sky and sea, rivers and lakes, and wild flowers, in particular—consists of varying shades of blues and whites. And second, conditionings formed from underlying mystical, or romantic, or pragmatic reasons, whichever way you happen to look at them, that have for so long connected blue and white with the heavens, the afterlife, eternity, infinity, and various virtues (and virtuous, saintly people like the Virgin Mary).

The predominately blue and white Chinese room at Claydon House, Buckinghamshire, England, is a splendid example of the extremely fanciful eighteenth-century English chinoiserie.

HEAVENLY BLUES

This is not so farfetched. The esoteric Chinese tradition, for example, certainly connected blue with immortality. Early Chinese emperors worshipped the blue sky, or the sky when it was blue, for this very reason, and rather fittingly, wore blue to do so. Tibetan Buddhist monks depicted wisdom and awareness (which they clearly took to be the same thing) as a brilliant blue. The ancient Greeks associated the color with "the sacred meeting place between earth and sky." Early Egyptians thought blue represented virtue, faith, and truth and wore the color for ceremonial mourning, which was not such a "downer" considering how much the Egyptians prized the afterlife as a death more living than life. In East Africa, blue represented (and with some tribes still represents) fertility and the joy of birth. And, slightly more prosaically, the Syrians wound blue string around the furry, often white, necks of their more precious domestic animals to protect them from death.

In the sixteenth century, Andrea Palladio, most masterly of ancient architects, gave white, too, a certain professional spirituality by deeming it "particularly satisfying to God." (This stricture was obviously taken up with a fervor, not necessarily religious, by early twentieth-century architects who made white—though not very often with blue—the *de rigueur* background for interiors. "White on white" was also the new look espoused in the 1920s and '30s by the fashionable decorators—Syrie Maugham, Elsie de Wolfe, and Basil Ionides. Although Oscar Wilde, always at the forefront of fashion, had been going on about the glories of white in his enthusiastically effete manner in the 1890s, when the Aesthetic Movement was at its height, and collections of blue and white Oriental porcelain were brought right back in to favor.)

The associations between blue, eternity, and immortality, blue and Heaven, heavenly blue and sky, and white and purity, godliness, and eventually cleanliness, seems to have continued down through the centuries. "Blue color is everlastingly appointed by the Deity to be a source of delight," expounded John Ruskin, the great Victorian art critic, in an 1853 lecture on art and architecture. (Incidentally, Ruskin only allowed his students at The Working Men's College to paint with Prussian blue—a deep, cool blue which was actually the first true chemical dye and color made from a compound of ferrocyanide. It was called "Prussian" because it was accidentally discovered in 1704, in Berlin, then the capital of Prussia, by a German chemist named Diesbach, and marketed from 1724.)

NATURAL BLUES AND WHITES

Actually, since so much of nature consists of sky and sea and inland waters, with their infinite variations of blue and white, it is scarcely surprising that the connection between blue and white and the mysteries of the heavens above and the afterlife are so entwined and so enduring.

> Then the sea
> And Heaven rolled as one and from the two
> Came fresh transfigurings of freshest blue

wrote the poet Wallace Stevens (1879–1955) in his

Extraordinarily beautiful and detailed figured blue and white tiles cover the walls and vaulted ceiling of the ancient Peninha chapel in Sintra, Portugal.

Sea Surface Full of Clouds, 1923.

To form one's own transfigurings, one has only to think of white light seeping up from a pale blue-gray dawn; the azure flecked with white of a high summer's day; the grapey blue and eerie white of impending storms; the deep velvety damson-blue surrounding the white moon of a scented night. Then think, as well, of the clear aquamarine of sun-dazzled water tipped with foam; the sparkling profundity of sapphire waves breaking against bleached rocks; the translucent turquoise of warmed sea gently lapping at white sand; spruce white sails on a still bluejohn lake. Such inspiration, which comes literally and perpetually from above and around, must surely become endemic, part of one's subconscious, with or without spiritual intimations. Nor can it be a coincidence—the availability of appropriate pigments and vegetable dyes apart—that so many combinations of blue and white in early mosaics, tiles, ceramics, and religious art came from Mediterranean, Middle Eastern, Oriental, African, Indian, Southern and Central American countries, where bright blue skies and deeper blue seas, white dust and whiter sand are a near constant background.

ANCIENT TONES

Differing permutations of blue and white, then, seem to be as old as the history of decorating. But although deeply prized, they were very far from common. While white, derived from lead pigment, was a much-used color with almost all the ancients, especially the Chinese, Greeks, and Romans, blues were the rarest and most expensive of pigments to produce. Their scarcity continued to the mid-nineteenth century, when chemists developed a whole range of synthetic dyes to replace the old mineral and vegetable colors. Nor was Palladio's white, "so satisfying to God," the pristine color (or, to be strictly accurate, noncolor, for neither black nor whites, grays, or browns, or neutrals are considered *real* colors) that we know and love and use so lavishly today. White was not made so crisp and brilliant until World War I, when it was transformed by the use of titanium dioxide.

The first blues were either extracted from minerals like lapis lazuli, cobalt, azurite, turquoise, and a copper compound like malachite mixed with various carbonates and silica, or from plants and shrubs like indigo and woad. Apparently, the semiprecious stone lapis lazuli, a warm delphinium-like blue with tiny golden flecks of crystals, was first used in conjunction with white marble and stone in Sumerian mosaics as far back as 3000 B.C. It was certainly to be seen in the Tutankhamen treasures. And dots of it, no more, were found in exquisitely-crafted game boards made of wood with inlaid mosaic decorations of bleached white bone, fragments of shells, and a red paste, excavated from the royal cemetery in Ur of the Chaldees, the biblical home of Abraham, and about where Iraq is now.

At that time, lapis, then only available from Afghanistan and the Sinai desert (with trade and communications being only as fast as primitive sailing boats and camels could make them), far from being semiprecious, was considered to be as desirable as gold. And even after it was discovered by the larger world, when it was introduced to medieval Europe via Sicily in the twelfth century, it continued to be rarified. Used as a pigment, it was such an expensive favorite for portraying both Italian skies and the robes of the Virgin Mary by great Renaissance painters from Duccio to Fra Filippo Lippi, to Raphael and Bellini, and Titian and Leonardo da Vinci, that the price of the paint was quoted separately to patrons and considered a status symbol, a most desirable extra.

Lapis was used to make what we call ultramarine blue (from the Italian *azzuro oltremarino* or literally, "blue from beyond the sea"), which was prepared by mixing grindings from the stone with egg white to produce a lovely liquid delphinium-like color. Although the same shade began to be reproduced artificially from 1828, nothing quite replaced the rich sparkle of the original, which continued to be highly desirable. The novelist and Yale lecturer, Alexander Theroux, who has made himself something of an authority on the color blue in general, has an Oxford University story of the Pre-Raphaelite painter Dante Gabriel Rossetti and the precious pot of paint. Rossetti, Edward Burne-Jones, and William Morris were painting a mural for the Oxford Union when Rossetti carelessly knocked over a whole potful of specially stipulated liquid lapis, leaving the hugely expensive beautiful pool of blue to leak messily through the floorboards, and the committee in charge of paying for the mural quite horrified. That there *is* even a story about a spilled paint pot so many years after the fact only goes to prove the regard in which such literally liquid blue chip assets were held.

Cobalt, an intense hyacinth blue and a compound of cobalt oxide, aluminum oxide, and phosphoric acid, although specially known as the "Ming" or "Nanking" blue the Chinese used from A.D. 1300 for their spectacular underglazed blue-and-white porcelain, was actually first used to color glass in Mesopotamia as far back as 2000 B.C. Its name, however, is derived from the fourteenth-century "Kobold," an evil demon supposed to haunt the mines where hundreds of workers died from what we now know must have been arsenic fumes from the ore.

Azurite, a singing sky-blue mineral derivative of copper, which we would call azure, was originally called "Armenian" blue by the ancient Roman writer Pliny, because it was mined there as well as in Spain. Since it was more local, so to speak, than the exotic lapis that had to come from Afghanistan or Egypt, it was often used as a substitute for the lapis-originated ultramarine by less prosperous painters. We do know, though, that the Spanish painter El Greco used it for the sky in his *Christ Driving The Traders From The Temple*. It was also a favorite color for Renaissance frescoes but apparently irritatingly elusive, for there are many recorded complaints from the time, that azurite, when mixed with water and applied to fresh damp plaster (which frescoing was all about), made the blue turn green. The remedy, apparently, was to mix it with a binder and to paint it on *dry* plaster.

Turquoise, the blue-green precious stone first

imported, like lapis lazuli, from the Sinai desert, is not only associated with ancient Egypt and Persia, but with a great many other ancient cultures from Tibet and India, to the Aztecs and Incas of Central and South America, who used it for religious masks as well as for tiles on domestic buildings. It was also widely used as a pigment to color Islamic and Mughal ceramics and was not unlike the brilliant caeruleum, then called "Egyptian" blue (because it was invented in Alexandria), but now known as cerulean, introduced by the Victorians as a chemical dye in the late 1850s. The original caeruleum was a blue glass made in ancient Egypt by firing, at high heat, a paste of silica, a copper compound like the vivid green malachite, calcium carbonate and natron, and a hydrated sodium carbonate. The glass was then crushed to form a pigment; the more coarse the grinding, the richer the blue. The pigment was also used by the Greeks, who called it *kyanos*, hence cyan, the blue in the poison cyanide.

BLUE AND WHITE IN EARLY INTERIORS

Although it is exceedingly rare to find extant examples or even fragments of really early interiors, there are some vivid descriptions and excellent documentation from contemporary writers that provide salient facts. In ancient Rome, it appears that blue and white were widely used for the often quite dazzling wall and ceiling mosaics, so fashionable after the development of concrete made the vaulting of ceilings possible. Marcus Vitruvius, a contemporary of the poet Virgil (70–19 B.C.) and the first great architectural critic, wrote the treatise *De Architectura*, which had such a profound effect some fifteen hundred years later on Renaissance artists like Alberti and Palladio. In it, Vitruvius not only describes the formation of the new caeruleum blue, but he describes how it was used, along with white twisted glass rods and white marble chips for mosaic walls in the Emperor Hadrian's villa at Tivoli, east of Rome. He also describes white marble chips set into painted blue plaster for an alternative wall treatment.

Many shades of blues, whites, and creams were also used for some of the famous ancient Roman frescoes that can still, thanks to stunning archaeological discoveries, be seen in museums and on preserved sites. In the Museo Nazionale Romano in Rome, for example, there is a delectable fresco from the first century B.C., said to have been removed from the house of the redoubtable Livia, wife of the Emperor Augustus (and villainess of the late Robert Graves's PBS series, *I, Claudius*). It is a garden scene, painted mainly in blues and blue-greens with a painted ivory-white wall acting as a dado or wainscoting beneath, which only goes to show that even the exquisitely wicked can still have exquisite taste. And a wall discovered in Pompeii, painted a warm, deep blue, overlaid with mythical figures, birds, and flowers, is subtly offset by delicate white and gold detailing. This design so beguiled the German Neoclassical architect Karl Friedrich Schinkel, in the early nineteenth century, that he reproduced it in his famous Schloss Charlottenhof in Potsdam, East Germany.

Although there are many descriptions of fabrics on chairs, couches, tables, and as wall and bed hangings by Homer, Pliny, and other Greek and Roman writers, the limitations imposed by the early scarcity of animal and vegetable dyes, as well as minerals, for pigments meant that at first very few blues were used for soft furnishings. These few were mainly derived from the deep dye of the indigo plant, called by the Romans "color Indicus," the color from India. (It also must have been available in the Philippines, because Manila, the name of the capital, comes from the Sanskrit, *nila,* meaning indigo, and the Manila bay area was famous for the dye that produced a beautiful morning glory color.) Indigo plants were also steeped in vats to produce the classic blue dye which we now use for denim, hence, too, the term "vat dye."

Although Homer described the piercingly blue Aegean sea as "wine-dark," he was obviously in no way color-blind, because he also describes at some length in the *Odyssey* the "deep blue wool" filling the work basket of the beautiful Helen of Troy (who one does not much imagine sewing or knitting away), which "ran on castors and was made of silver finished with a rim of gold." Homer talks, too, of the soft purply blue blankets on the guest bed in King Menelaus's palace.

THE BYZANTINE INFLUENCE

Apart from the classical architecture, designs, and writings of ancient Greece and Rome, the other great influence from this period was Byzantium: the Byzantine Empire, formerly the Eastern Greek Empire, which spread through Greece to the Middle East and on through to the Black Sea and North Africa. It was a huge area, with an equally huge number of cross-cultural influences, which became the Eastern Roman Empire from A.D. 476 to 1453, when it fell to the Turks. The very word Byzantine evokes the image of a sophisticated, particularly luxurious sumptuousness. Unfortunately, nothing remains to be seen of Byzantine Constantinople, now the city of Istanbul, the city that the Roman and first Christian emperor, Constantine, made his capital and to which he gave his name. But Byzantine architecture and interiors were known for their exotic coloring and sybaritic comfort, and there are lyrical descriptions of interiors including one in a tenth-century poem. It tells of semiprecious blue stones (probably lapis lazuli again) used with rock crystal for extravagant floor mosaics, along with white marble walls and windows set with alabaster, cut so thinly that the resulting pure white light gave the illusion of living in the heart of a glacier.

Much of the Byzantine sumptuousness was imported into Venice, the south of Italy, and Sicily in the tenth and eleventh centuries. Artistic and luxury-loving doges of Venice, princes of southern Italy, and the Norman kings of Sicily, all men of sophisticated tastes, hired teams of Byzantine craftsmen to enrich their palaces, great houses, and churches. The most beautiful, purely Byzantine interiors surviving in Western Europe are to be seen in Palermo, Sicily, at the La Ziza (Arabic for splendid) and Cuba Palaces, now, alas, in a very poor state of repair, and in the heavily restored *Salon di*

Ruggero in the Royal Palace, or Palace of the Normans. In the latter, there is a luxurious but subtly colored mixture of pale blue and white marble for the floor and lower walls, with elaborate mosaics on the upper walls and vaulted ceiling of flowers and trees, birds and animals, in pale blues, blue-greens, white, and gold.

The deeply luxurious influence on design and decoration provided by Byzantium was also carried all over the Muslim world and then back again into Western Europe from another quarter, when Arabs and Berbers from Morocco swept across what is now the Strait of Gibraltar into Spain. The new fanatically religious but highly artistic Islamic–Moorish–Spanish civilization that arose from this Arabic conquest was centered around the southern Spanish cities of Córdoba, Seville, and Granada. But it is the great fortress–palace of the Alhambra, bestriding the ravine that divides Granada, that is not only the most spectacular of all European palaces, but one of the world's finest examples of the sustained use of blue and white.

Although the Alhambra was constructed over several centuries, it was substantially rebuilt, renovated, and refurbished between 1309 and 1354 by Abd-el-Walid and his successors, who might well be thought of, had they been Christians, as the patron saints of blue and white. For it is their spectacularly decorated structure that we still see today, with its tiles of mainly blue and white (with touches of apricot-yellow, terracotta, rose-reds, and greens) covering pillars, fountains, floors, walls, and ceilings. Water still cascades from blue and white tiled

fountains and trickles down from blue and white tiled basins into similarly tile-lined pools and canals that meander through leafy courtyards and back into gracefully pillared rooms. Indeed, the transition between outer courtyards and inner reception rooms is barely discernible with the intricate patterns of sun-dappled boughs and leaves outside, repeated in the splendid tile work within.

The Moorish occupation of Spain lasted until 1492, the year that the Italian Christopher Columbus, financed by Spain, discovered America. The two events had nothing whatsoever to do with each other except to presage the new order of things. The Moorish rulers of the magnificent Alhambra were forced to surrender to King Ferdinand of Castile and Queen Isabella of Aragon. Nor were the Moors able to extend their influence to France, Britain, Italy, or the Netherlands, for the mountain ranges of the Pyrenees, together with deep religious differences, created too much of a divide. But the blue and white tiles and pottery used in and on so many old buildings in Spain and Portugal and, of course, North Africa and the Middle East are a lasting legacy along with all those old movie houses, which, in an effort to sound suitably exotic, called themselves Alhambras. There are also blue, white, and terracotta Spanish tiles called alambrillas, named after an Alhambra floor pattern.

THE CHURCH AS PATRON

The European feudal system that followed the Graeco-Roman, Byzantine, and Moorish influences via the French Norman occupation was as

Elaborate nineteenth-century blue and white (and occasionally yellow) tile work is carefully distributed over windows and doors on the façade of a Portuguese house.

different in its attitude to color and comfort and general domestic civilization as scented silk is to coarse homespun. Since most of the ruling classes spent most of their time defending their own far-flung estates, or attacking their neighbors in order to sequester more land, almost all dwellings of any size were heavily fortified, and their occupants were perpetually on the move. There was little time to spend in any one home, let alone to beautify it, except with portable objects that could be transported from place to place, hence the French word for furniture *meuble,* meaning movable. But if domestic life was short on glamour, color, and comfort, the medieval Church more than compensated. Since it was rarely shy or slow in demanding its dues, the Church, at that time still unadulteratedly Catholic, had become enormously wealthy. Cathedrals, churches, chapels, monasteries, abbeys, and convents were more often than not lavishly decorated, since the princes of the Church could afford to patronize and commission architects, artists, and craftsmen in a way that few secular princes could rival.

The cult of the Blessed Virgin, the Mother of Christ, was extremely important in a Europe where, for the majority, religion was the most stable and comforting factor, the common denominator, the theater in their lives. And since both paintings and statues were invariably dressed mainly in blue and white, the combination of colors, and their association with goodness, was a major influence.

There were, of course, exceptions to the general lack of secular luxury, mainly in the later medieval courts of Spain, Portugal, and particularly France, some of whose interiors were so beautifully depicted in *Les Très Riches Heures du Duc de Berry.* These were the exquisitely illuminated manuscripts executed around 1415 for the powerful Duke of Berry, ruler of one of the richest provinces of France, by the gifted illuminators, the Limbourg brothers. Here there are many permutations of blue and white shown in room backgrounds, most strikingly in the "January" section, where the Duc de Berry himself is depicted sitting at a long trestle table with a white damask cloth set over a richly-worked dark blue undercloth, for all the world like an *Elle Decor* table setting. Another charming illumination from the late fifteenth century, *Les Heures Boucicaut,* shows a canopied bed with curtains of deep cornflower blue embroidered with gold *fleurs-de-lys.* And although there is no other white in the room except for a wide white ribbon gracefully encircling the top of the canopy, there is quite enough to make a statement.

The dye used for these deep blue fabrics was the very same woad mentioned by Julius Caesar in his *Conquest of Gaul,* which besmeared the ancient Celts and Britons. It was extracted from the leaves of the scrubby little woad plant, which was as much a scourge to the environment then as industrial pollution is today. Woad exhausted the land it grew on, and the numerous vats needed to extract the dye poisoned the air around them. But because the demand for blue cloth was so great, it became just as much of an unfortunate facet of life as today's damaging industrial pollution.

RENAISSANCE BLUES

During the fifteenth century, Europe became much more stable, less fractious, and generally more prosperous with, happily, a more equitable distribution of wealth. This new domestic stability was a blessing for every country, but in Italy it resulted in the splendid Renaissance, the rebirth of all the Greek and Roman classical ideals, so that the *quattrocento,* as it was called, became like the glorious Greek fifth century B.C. Rich and powerful families like the Medicis and the Gonzagas turned their energy, money, and esthetic sensibilities to making beautiful houses and patronizing the arts rather than making war, and great collections of paintings, sculptures, tapestries, blue and white ceramics, and furniture were accumulated. Generous patronage produced great architects and painters. But along with a passion for contemporary art, came an intense interest in the antique. And although remnants of classical interiors were not discovered until the eighteenth century, the writings of Vitruvius, with all their concise color descriptions and notes on design, were studied as eagerly as design magazines today. Wall surfaces not covered with paintings, tapestries, or hangings of tooled leather or cloth were usually frescoed, or covered with an interesting combination of fresco and stucco relief; and in rooms with very high ceilings, the upper part of the wall generally had some sort of decorative frieze. *Trompe l'œil* became very fashionable. Many walls were covered in garden or outdoor scenes complete with pergola canes and rampant vines like morning glory mixed with grapes, birds, and animals against blue skies, rather like the charming garden *trompe l'œil* commissioned by Livia fifteen centuries earlier. And all sorts of variegated and different-colored *faux* marbles were painted over whole expanses of plaster and floors, as well as for dadoes and moldings, so that almost every house of note, not to mention churches and cathedrals, had some sort of painted finish. On the whole, the grand interiors of the time were too complex and richly detailed to have much truck with the simplicity of only blue and white, but plenty of both colors was used in conjunction with others, and the combination was particularly utilized for the handsome *pietra Dura,* variegated stone-and-marble-top tables of the period, which were often inlaid with the costly lapis lazuli and bluejohn to a magnificent effect.

BAROQUE SKY BLUES

The Baroque period, which followed the Renaissance in Europe, started in Italy in the early seventeenth century and rapidly spread to Germany, Austria, Spain, Russia, Scandinavia, and, to some extent, England, but reached an apotheosis of a sort in France. Indeed, France, from that time until the nineteenth century, took over the mantle of Italy as the leader in design, with magnificent architects like Le Vau and magnificent palaces like Versailles. At this time, blue and white really became part of the accepted interior decoration in great houses, though mostly on ceilings, with cloud and sky scenes a favorite motif, overpainted with *putti,* cherubim, saints, and various less saintly

mortals. For example, the state bedroom at Chatsworth, the seat of the dukes of Devonshire, in Derbyshire, England, has just such a sky scene of the period, vigorously peopled, set above an immensely elaborate cornice equally crowded with carved cherubs and allegorical characters.

DUTCH COURAGE

It was really due to the Dutch that blue and white left the exclusive province of grand houses and came into the normal public realm, so to speak. Under Prince Maurice of Orange—a fairy-tale title, if ever there was one—little Holland became the major sea power in the world, with huge colonial possessions in the East and Africa. The Dutch East India Company, founded to trade with the Far East and the rest of the world, began to import a huge range of Chinese cobalt blue and white underglazed porcelains, peacock-colored silks, Japanese lacquered screens and other lacquered goods, fine jades, and exquisitely painted papers.

It so happened that at much the same time, in the middle of the seventeenth century, many French Protestants or Huguenots, as they were called, fled to Holland (and to England and America) after the Edict of Nantes forbade them to practice their religion in France. One of these Huguenots, Daniel Marot, famous for his furniture designs and interiors in France, was commissioned by King William of Orange to design the interior of the Royal Palace. Marot seized eagerly on the new blue and white Chinese porcelains as the key to his design schemes, and added to the blue and white theme by creating

chimney pieces with stepped supports for the Chinese pieces and blue *faïence* vases.

The impact of these rooms, with their collections of blue and white, was strong. Since there could hardly be enough of the Chinese porcelain for everyone who wanted it, the Dutch Delft pottery went into production with its own blue and white products: charming earthenware and tiles covered with opaque tin enamel and decorated with much the same cobalt blue that the Chinese used, but, in Holland, called Leyden blue after the Dutch town, Leyden. Taking advantage of the new wares, the interiors of the bourgeois homes became full of collections of blue and white porcelain and pottery set against white-painted walls, fireplaces inset with Delft tiles, and precise black and white marble-tiled floors. These kinds of interiors can be seen as backgrounds in many of the contemporary Dutch paintings of the period, by artists like Vermeer and Hans Vredeman de Vries.

When King William and his wife Queen Mary, by a quirk of fate, also took over the throne of England (where, with unusual sexual equality, they reigned as "William and Mary"), they again commissioned Marot, clearly the Mark Hampton of the time, to design rooms for them in Cardinal Wolsey's old palace of Hampton Court. There, in the handsome old Tudor building, Marot reintroduced his familiar chimney pieces, as well as blue and white tulip bulb stands and tiered flower pyramids. So the fashion for blue and white with Oriental porcelains and Delft earthenware spread to England, then to the rest of Europe, and finally to America,

This French *toile de Jouy* cotton, called "Le Ballon de Gonesse," records man's first flight in a balloon from the Champ-de-Mars in Paris to Gonesse in 1793.

whose citizens had begun to settle down to a more comfortable way of life after their pioneering privations. Indeed, so enamored were the Americans with the whole "William and Mary" look, that they went on with the style long after Queen Anne had ascended to the throne in England, and they sent their own boats to China with instructions to cram the holds with blue and white porcelain.

ROCOCO MASTERPIECES

Although the fashion for blue-and-white porcelain and earthenware became universally prevalent on both sides of the Atlantic in the late seventeenth century, it was not until the early eighteenth century and the advent of the Rococo style that *entire* blue and white rooms became universally popular in Europe. And again, of course, since blue pigment remained expensive, blue and white were mainly the province of the rich. The Rococo's light and airy look vanquished the heavy overmantels, the solid paneling, and the pilasters and pillars of the Baroque in favor of large expanses of mirror, lightly and airily carved paneling, delicate cornices and plasterwork, and deliberately light colors, particularly blue and ivory white, and rose and green, with an extravagant use of gilt. Chinoiserie, in the form of fantastic plasterwork in convoluted shapes, elaborate silks, lacquered screens, and splendid wallcoverings, imported by the enterprising Dutch East India Company, or copied from such imports, became extremely popular.

Although the Rococo did not much affect England, or, at that time, America (the look became very popular, indeed, in the late nineteenth century, when it became known as "the Louis Revival"), it spread very quickly to Italy, Scandinavia, Russia, and particularly to Germany and Austria. There are several splendid blue and white (and gold) Rococo rooms to be seen in Italy today, such as the extravagant Chinese Room in the Palazzo Reale in Turin and the quite extraordinary central saloon of the *Palazzina di Ceccia* at Stupinigi. Equally breathtaking is the Spiegelsaal, in the Amalienburg, Nymphenburg, Munich, Germany, originally built as a hunting lodge for the Electress Amelia by the great French architect François de Cuvilliés, the elder. Here, palest silvered carvings of flowers and fruit, vases, cartouches, *putti*, musical instruments, birds, and Chinese trellis work are all in relief against a white ceiling and soft blue walls. Even the frames of the furniture are elaborately silvered against sumptuous creamy ivory upholstery.

In England, where at the time Palladianism mixed with a little bit of the Baroque had combined to produce some of the most beautiful classical interiors to be seen, the one aspect of the Rococo that did find favor was chinoiserie. The fanciful blue and white Chinese room at Claydon House, Buckinghamshire, is well worth a visit for keen blue and white aficionados.

COLONIAL BLUES

In the meantime, Colonial settlers in America, with their mixed European antecedents, were evolving a charming and enduring style of their own, romanticized by the Neocolonialism of this century. This style consisted of elegantly simplified versions of European furniture, beguiling folk art, a whole series of rustic hutches and armoires, very often painted a soft, deep gray-blue (now thought of as "Colonial" blue, but based on the Prussian blue pigment), and a good deal of straightforward blue and white checkered cotton.

Another uniquely American blue that evolved at the time was the pale blue-green called "Apothecary" blue, after the ubiquitous large glass apothecary jars ranged in old pharmacy stores. This color was much used in the South, where it looked cool in the Southern sun, and was particularly popular in the town of Williamsburg, Virginia, where it is still to be seen.

One of the profound changes in the eighteenth century, in fact, was the spread of a kind of domesticated style, with national variations, of course, as the middle classes became increasingly more prosperous. In America, France, Spain, Portugal, Italy, Scandinavia, Britain, the Netherlands, and even South Africa, small provincial farm and country houses inspired a rural style of their own, which often included blue and white tiles, blue and white ceramics and pottery, painted floors, furniture, and paneling, as well as a lot of checkered and French *toile de Jouy* fabrics. Town houses, of course, were more sophisticated but considerably more informal than the grander houses of the upper classes.

NEOCLASSICAL BLUES

The other landmark events for design in general and blue and white in particular were the thrilling archaeological discoveries of classical remains and parts of rooms in Pompeii and Herculaneum, and later in Greece and Sicily. These discoveries revealed a totally unsuspected ancient sophistication and technical efficiency, quite apart from a coloring expertise, that stimulated the collective imagination. People in many countries were delighted with the deep brilliant blues of painted plaster, the azure blues and blue-greens of frescoes, and the blue and white mosaics and pavement tiles. Neoclassicism, the style the discoveries engendered, was the first real International Style.

In England, the elegant Robert Adam, sometimes known as "Bob, the Roman" because of his predilection for all things classical and ancient, Roman in particular, had his early work somewhat rudely described as "snippets of embroidery." It was so described because of its lightness and ease after the grandeur of Palladian interiors, which were so full of pediments and pilasters, and architraves and columns. But he was a great exponent of blue and white, as can be seen by many of his great houses, now open to the public. The dining room at Nostell Priory, in Yorkshire, for example, is subtly blue and white, with gently painted wall panels in the softest blue outlined with white, and a highly decorative brighter blue and white ceiling. His anteroom at Syon House, just outside London, is a spectacular example of blue tones on tone with blue-gray and white spiced up with cerulean, azure and ultramarine, and a contrast of terracotta. Adam espoused the Roman variety of Classicism, and so did the Americans, who seized upon the discovery of the

ancient architecture of Republican Rome (never mind the lapse to Imperial Rome and the mainly corrupt reigns of the Roman emperors) as a fitting representation of their own recently won freedom, but called it Federal.

In France, however, early Neoclassicism was called *Le Goût Grec*—an early forerunner of the later American Greek Revival style—and had, as one of its leading exponents, the architect Ange-Jacques Gabriel. One of Gabriel's most charming and harmonious classical buildings is *le Petit Trianon* at Versailles, which again provided a kind of landmark for domestic architecture. All the major rooms are decorated in soft blue-grays, blues, and whites, and, because of their relatively small scale, were considered elegantly comfortable rather than grand, a state most sensible people aspired to from then on. Gabriel's newly evolved style, with its pastel colors, restrained cornices and moldings, simple paneling, and large plain overmantel mirrors, became enormously popular. "One lives in a comfort unknown to our parents and not yet attained by other nations," commented Voltaire in a somewhat self-satisfied way. He was wrong. The future third President of the United States of America and then ambassador to France, Thomas Jefferson, was equally enamored, and had carried

Stylized Oriental porcelain mythical beasts are massed dramatically on a marble ledge in a Kip's Bay, New York City, showhouse.

out just such comfortably charming schemes in his own graceful Virginian house, Monticello, a house that was to become an elegant dream to aspire to for many Americans.

CHINA BLUES

Perhaps the final contribution of the eighteenth century to the popularity of blue and white was the spate of new porcelain factories and potteries producing the two-color ware, as well as the flood of Japanese porcelains and the Chinese export designs, manufactured especially by the prescient Chinese, complete with appropriate motifs, for both European and American markets.

In England, Staffordshire pottery finally found a white-bodied enough ware to decorate with blue and its designs and romantic scenes became collectors' treasures in no time at all. Wedgwood produced its unique grayed blue backgrounds with white relief; both Minton and Worcester produced their wonderful variegated blues on white; and the much beloved "Chinese" blue and white willow pattern plates and services were churned out for the general public, who have been buying them ever since. In France, the royal porcelain factory at Sèvres copied the piercing turquoise blue used for so long by the Persians. French porcelain manufacturers were also famous for the deep, rich royal blue background that they used for many of their fragile porcelain ornaments and dinner services, and for their *bleu céleste,* not surprisingly translated as sky blue, or heavenly blue, another version of cerulean, which was first developed in 1772.

TRAVELERS' TALES

The "Grand Tour," extended voyages of cultural discovery by well-to-do European gentlemen, had long been a fact of the eighteenth century. But by the nineteenth century, as travel became easier and colonialism more rampant, more people ventured further afield for work as well as pleasure. Indian, Far Eastern, and African ideas were brought back to both America and Europe, and people marveled over the exotic architecture and colors of North Africa, the East, and, in particular, India. The British Prince Regent's Brighton Pavilion is a prime example. Here the exotic blues of India were widely used, and the daring Banqueting Room with its blue sky-domed ceiling, immense white flower petal chandeliers, bright blue walls, and white-painted inset panels of Indian scenes, outlined with red and gilt *faux* bamboo frames, must have had a dazzling effect at the time, just as it dazzles still.

Soldier's tales, too, were an important factor. Napoleon's Egyptian campaign created an important addition to the nineteenth-century French Empire, English Regency, American Federal, and later, American Empire styles. Spoken and written descriptions, and subsequent illustrations, created a new fashion for Egyptian sphinxes, palm trees, and Nubian and Nefertiti-like figures, quite apart from the often blue and white striped tent-like rooms and campaign-like furniture. Egyptian blue, the original bright cerulean blue, became a favorite color of the Regency, Empire, and Federal periods, as did a lavender blue, probably derived from mixing Prussian blue with rose.

NEW DYES, PIGMENTS, AND SHADES

In tune with all these exotic advances in design ideas were tremendous technical advances in synthetic dye and pigment-making, which produced a much larger palette of colors to be used in fabrics and paints. At first, it is true, the colors were harsh, almost brazen—vegetable dyes are still the gentlest—but manufacturers learned to soften and vary them in comparatively few years, so that a whole galaxy of new blues became available.

Although mid- and late nineteenth-century interiors tended, for the most part, to be darker and heavier than earlier color schemes, by the turn of the century the Aesthetic Movement and the Arts and Crafts Movement, on both sides of the Atlantic, not only brought back lighter, airier colors, and a great choice of them, but also revived an interest in the Orient, particularly Japan, as well as Oriental blue and white porcelains. To hold often massive collections of blue and white, it became the fashion to inset shelves just below the cornice of a room.

The Arts and Crafts Movement, and to some extent Art Nouveau, produced many blue-and-white interiors, notably the famous entrance hall of the now classic Scottish Hill House at Helensburgh, overlooking the Clyde River, designed by Charles Rennie Mackintosh. Other examples include Whistler's notorious Peacock Room, now in Washington's Freer Gallery, and several elaborately tiled interiors by the Englishman Halsey Ricardo. In fact, a new Moorish influence, with a great deal of complicated blue and white tile work, Mooresque carvings, and mosaics, was much in evidence in both prosperous London and New York homes at the turn of the century.

PAINTERLY LAST WORDS

Just as painters were a great influence on the colors of the Renaissance, so, too, were painters of the late-nineteenth and early-twentieth centuries. Pre-Raphaelites, Impressionists, Fauvists, Cubists, the Blue Rose group of 1907, in Russia, and the *Blaue Reiter* group, founded in Germany in 1911, all either used a good many blue and white combinations or wrote about them glowingly. Matisse's *Blue Nude* on cream was actually much the same color that he used for his dazzling stained glass windows against white walls in his chapel in Venice. "Blue is heavenly, pure and infinite, suggestive of eternal peace," wrote Kandinsky, the joint founder of the *Blaue Reiter* group. "The deeper blue becomes," he added in his *On the Spiritual in Art,* "the more urgently it summons man towards the infinite, the more it arouses in him a longing for purity and, ultimately, the supersensual." Blue is still being allied with the eternal, even in the twentieth century, although one cannot imagine that all the owners of dark blue rooms have that in mind.

Given the history of blues and whites, their tenacious spiritual connections, and the delight in the fact that something formerly so rare can now be had in as many permutations as nature itself, it is hardly surprising that the combination *is* so loved. And it will presumably continue to be loved, not just for tradition's sake, but for the fact that it does provide such a sense of peace and cheerful calm.

Rare blue and white porcelains were given pride of place on shelves above the paneled chimney piece in King George II's private chamber at Hampton Court Palace near London.

The Hallway and Stairway

No one would dispute that, in the best of all possible worlds, hallways should be welcoming or that corridors and stairways can provide interesting backgrounds for collections, and that both spaces should try to convey some sense of the rest of the home. Occasionally, of course, a spectacular architectural triumph of a staircase *(opposite),* or a particularly beautifully detailed and proportioned space will stand on its own. But most often color and decoration of whatever sort are the medium relied upon to cheer up these often neglected spaces acting as a background for paintings, prints, and objects.

Certainly, judiciously used, versatile blues and whites with all their varied range of tones and possible permutations, are admirably suited to the task, adding brightness and freshness to sometimes not very light areas; or a sense of cool stillness to a summer house or house in the sun. Equally, deep, jewel-tone blues can be relied upon to show off white or light-painted architectural details, or prized collections, in a most distinguished way, while soft, washed-out blues and slightly yellowed whites can add a sense of noble, faded grandeur to underscore the obvious age of a house.

Welcoming azure blues, airy blues and whites, soft gray-blues acting as gentle backgrounds for furniture of disparate periods, deep, handsome blues, old tile blues, joyful blues like patches of captured sky, varying tones of blues, like lilacs and hyacinths, violets and periwinkles, forget-me-nots, lupins, and delphiniums, hydrangeas and scabious or cornflowers, again used together with soft white for greater liveliness... Or a great bursting vase of rich blue flowers in season against pure white walls....All these delectable combinations are undeniably useful for creating pleasurable entrances and memorable exits. Nor, once more, should one underestimate the pleasure of seeing collections of blue and white porcelain or earthenware assembled on walls, or balanced on shelves to light up odd corners.

andsome stylized floral tiles are used to form a deep and impressive dado with unusual scalloped edges. They also balance the exuberantly-curved and painted cornice in the predominantly blue hallway of a newly restored 1912–1915 villa in Cadaqués, Northern Spain. Small scale, neatly geometric, blue and white floor tiles make a crisp contrast to all the other exotica. This is reinforced by the glowing hyacinth blue paint used for doors, window frames, and muntins, which, with their disciplined straight lines, add a needed counterpoint to all the elaborate patterns and curves.

Few blue lovers would argue the fact that white makes a natural background for blue and white porcelain and earthenware (as well, of course, for a variety of other objects). But there is something about blue and white china set against blue, whether pale or dark, bright or subtle, that makes for a peculiarly satisfying combination. It is as if the blue and white designs are suspended in a quiet blue space specifically for our better contemplation. Certainly, this observation is particularly well illustrated by this hallway vignette in an eighteenth-century French château *(above),* where the combination of the nineteenth-century Chinese ginger jars, the magnificent nineteenth-century urn, the colors of the flowers, the elaboration of the carved eighteenth-century side table, and the tracery of the paneling is all set off by the palest blue-gray of the wall behind. The London staircase and hallway *(right)* could hardly provide a greater contrast of styles, but here, too, the essentially blue background, relieved by the white and black marble, provides the same kind of contemplative background for the very different shapes of the Mackintosh Art Nouveau chair and complicatedly curving balustrade, the ornate nineteenth-century mirror, and the splayed crystal-armed light fixture hung high over the staircase.

Tawny marble floors and a particularly handsome white-painted double staircase *(left)* are enhanced by deep Prussian blue walls, as, of course, is the collection of blue and white Staffordshire English plates hung above the large nineteenth-century painting on the halfway landing. The wicker baskets stashed with lavender and pinecones under the stairs are something of a leavening touch in an otherwise rather grand and formal space in an Algarve, Portugal, villa de-signed by David Hicks. A series of neatly gilt-framed intaglios *(above)*, mounted on cobalt blue velvet, are hung against blue and white ribbon rosettes on a soft blue-gray and white staircase wall in a Victorian house in London. The pale blue painted wrought iron banis-ters, surmounted by an elegantly curved mahogany rail, are an unexpected but felicitous touch against the dark blue of the stair carpet and the blue and white curtains with their blue-fringed tiebacks.

Soft sky blue has been imaginatively used *(left)* to both outline and domesticate the Gothic arches in the arresting hallway of St. Michael's Mount, Cornwall, England. Notice how subtly the various geometric shapes blend into one another: the octagonal panels on the double doors, the striking double diamonds of the tiled floor, the elongated diamonds of the window panes, not to mention the Gothic tracery of the Regency chairs, echoing the gracefully soaring arches above. A beautifully hung collection of nineteenth-century portrait plates *(top)* turns an otherwise plain little hall into something of a show-stopper in a New York City apartment. The blue plate rims meld softly into the *faux*-painted rustic block wall.

31

An interesting mixture of cobalt blue and turquoise in a London home, designed by Steve Ibbotson for Andrew Wadsworth *(left)*, forms a brilliant frame for the rather somber room beyond. Such contrasts of light and shade, brilliance and sobriety, are the spice of a house and can be particularly apposite in a hallway, emphasizing as here, the coolness of the dining room beyond. The very pale hallway *(right)*, in an ancient former château in Normandy, France, now used as an inn, is in direct contrast to the vivid coloring opposite, but the blue, soft though it is, is used to maximum effect. Notice the arresting blue-painted patches on the worn tiled floor that look like Neanderthal footprints that, for some reason, stop almost as soon as they begin.

Neat little blue and white checkered tiles are used to line the stairs, the floor, and the blue-edged plunge pool in the exotic pool room of a Spanish house. The vivid cornflower blue triple arches, surrounded by an extraordinary border of blue relief and white tiles, make an arresting division between the plunge bath and the romantically flower-edged and balustraded *trompe l'œil* painted swimming pool next door. The blueness and coolness of this subterranean area is further exaggerated by the literally electric blue light illuminating the overscale blue-silk plant in its capacious bright blue pottery bowl.

One of the most charming of all the charming Neoclassical manifestations in the late eighteenth–early nineteenth centuries was the Gustavian period in Sweden. Colors were light and airy, lines were crisp, Neoclassical motifs were subtly interpreted, and a great deal of the decorational effect on furniture, as well as walls, was achieved with the clever use of paint. The Gustavian blue and white panelled door and walls in Tido Castle, Sweden, shown here, is an excellent example of the genre. Note the Neoclassical garland of laurel leaves over the door, the twisted Greek key border (a new variation on the classic theme), and the acanthus leaf medallions.

A gently subfusc blue and white stenciled design *(left),* painted by Peter Farlow for Mimmi O'Connell, covers the landing outside as well as the bedroom walls and door to soften angles and edges. The hazy overall pattern is sharply placed in focus by the brighter blue and white striped rug and the honey-colored chair. An equally subfusc effect has been made by the marble *faux* finish wallpaper of the staircase and hall walls *(right).* It makes an effective background for the gracefully graphic stone staircase, the elegant stair rails, and the long shuttered windows of this French house. The wallpaper, in fact, is so decorative that it stands on its own without benefit of art of any sort.

The Living Room

Of all the rooms in a home, the living room is the space that is most often on show to others, the room that is most visited, the room that displays one's tastes and interests to other people. But it is also the room that has to accommodate the requirements of all members of the family, unless a home is large with alternatives like guest rooms, family rooms, dens, dining rooms, playrooms, studies, libraries, and media rooms. That is to say, unless you have the luxury of a room entirely devoted to formal entertaining, there generally needs to be adequate but good-looking storage for books and tapes, CDs and videos, probably drinks, and possibly toys (or, at least, concealing space for the toys left behind after play), quite apart from space for the display of art and objects.

There often has to be a desk or writing table, or a dining table, or a table that does double duty for both; space for a computer and most often a television, VCR, and stereo speakers. Above all, however elegant, interestingly eclectic, well-planned, and practical the room is, it also has to be comfortable to be a successful living room, a room for living in.

Comfort is not just a question of good upholstery and plenty of pillows. Comfort is also good lighting in which to read and to view paintings, objects, and books on bookshelves. It is some sort of table space by every seat—or as many seats as possible—somewhere to put your feet up when you can really relax; and colors and textures that are easy on the eye. And remember: If beauty lies in the eye of the beholder, comfort lies in the sensations of the user.

Given blue's calming and refreshing propensities, I have always found it a good background color for living rooms, whether using a cheerful sky blue with white for woodwork and any moldings, and white, or blue and white in different textures and patterns for window treatments and soft furnishings. Or using aquamarine, say, for walls, ceiling, and curtains with white woodwork and moldings, cooled in summer by white flowers and large green plants; warmed in winter by red or pink flowers, fire, and lamplight. Conversely, backgrounds can be white with blue, with blue and white soft furnishings; or a very dark blue and cream with lighter blues. There are so many permutations on the blue and white theme, so little to get tired of, and it is certainly both comfortable and comforting to look at.

"Summer afternoon—Summer afternoon," as Henry James was supposed to have remarked, "to me have always been the two most beautiful words in the English language." And certainly this airy room near Boston, Massachusetts, belonging to painter Michel Pouliot, looks decorated for precisely that. The cool antithesis for a hot blue day. Of course, when summer has slipped by, and the emphasis on cool is no longer desirable, the crisp white throws come off the textured oatmeal upholstery and the room, while still substantially blue and white, assumes a new warmth, a different direction. With the tawny floor and playful terracotta-painted side table under the window its new focus, it proves that moods in a room can, with a little forethought, be changed as easily as the moods of the sky. Note, too, how the height of the plinth holding the plant gives balance, along with the tall painting by the window, to the otherwise low level and mostly "found" furnishings in the rest of the room.

Blues of every kind were highly fashionable during the late-eighteenth and early-nineteenth century Regency period in England, mainly due to returning travelers' tales of the exotic blues to be found in India. Another great favorite style of the time was Gothic, which, along with chinoiserie, appealed to the fanciful tastes of the time. Both colors and style, then, were appropriate choices for the decoration of the room *(above),* in St. Michael's Mount, Cornwall, England, a gloriously romantic Gothic building perched craggily on top of rocks at the edge of the Irish Sea. The deeper tone of the curtain design (beautifully made with Gothicized white-fringed and -bordered pelmet and palest blue lining) makes a dramatic frame for the cerulean blue and white camel-backed sofa, which reflects, in turn, the walls. The extremely dark blue, almost black, walls in the dramatic Victorian library cum dining room *(right),* are relieved by the sky blue carpet and the densely-patterned and swagged curtains, as well as by the blue-green velvet on the Empire chair, and the Oriental lamp on the Regency mahogany and ebony writing table. Observe the esoteric still life of marble and gilt objects.

This high-ceilinged Mexican room in a colonial town house in Guernavaca is like a time warp from the nineteenth century, except for the group of comfortable modern chairs. The gamut of blues was carefully chosen to make the room, cluttered as it is, a cool retreat from the intense Mexican sun. It certainly works, especially with the addition of the pure white upholstery fabric and the airy sheers at the window.

Rooms full of careful detail, like this country living room on the Greek island of Patmos, belonging to Geneva architect Chantal Scaler, need to be lingered over to fully absorb the clever juxtapositions present. There are the varying tones of blue, the pale blue-whites of the upholstery, and the contrast of the wood colors from the rich chestnut of the ceiling beams to the ebony of the lacquered Empire style mirror and the modern seating frames of the local furniture. The heavily carved doors are painted a clear aqua, like the old Persian and Mughal empire blue, while the window frames and small campaign table are a definite azure. The pair of country corner cabinets, with their collections of blue and white ceramics and Bristol blue glass, are painted a shiny cerulean blue. And the floorboards are painted a definite lavender. Disparate as all these tones are, they meld together in happy harmony to give the long room a kind of cool peace.

Although there are no architectural details of any interest in the corner of this French living room, near Nantes, or in the corridor beyond, the area is nevertheless made to look quite striking by the subtle use of a gamut of mauvey-blues. They range from the violet of the stained floorboards, to the pale amethyst of the corridor, to the pinky rubbed blue of the living room wallpaper and general woodwork. Naturally, with such a deliberate build-up of one color, the blue damask of the little nineteenth-century slipper chair, in the foreground, melds right into the general blue haze. It is relieved only by the ivory reveals of the windows and the odd roses among the vase of cornflowers. Interestingly, in the absence of any art, the deliberate play on blues becomes a kind of graphic art in itself.

Romantically worn azure blue walls in a French villa make a spectacular foil for a collection of old black and white photographs of the glory days of the Raj. (Interestingly, India's ancient princes took up photography in the very early days, for in their palaces all over the country there are similar collections proudly displayed.) The Shiite glass object and old stone on top of the gray and white marble tabletop tone in gently with the general patchiness. This same blue, a legacy of the Mughal empire and a suitable background for Indian objects, is favored as much for its cooling propensities as for the bright intensity of its tone, which manages to staunchly hold its own against the pervasive sun.

Eighteenth-century Delft ginger jars *(left)*, along with an equally beautifully decorated pot, are balanced by elegantly draped blue and white curtains caught up by a deep blue ribbon. Notice how the freshness of the blues and whites highlights the gentle coloring of the faded old paneling and the eighteenth-century statue on its white marble plinth.

Much the same feeling is evoked in another elegant French house *(left)*, with its two-tone stone-painted paneling, which matches the eighteenth-century stone fireplace and floor and the bleached, carved late eighteenth-century writing table and chairs, in a conscious monotone. Against this subtle pallor, the clear blue and white of the curtains, armchair, and daybed virtually sing out. Look, too, at the blue and white detail of the nineteenth-century French ceramic chickens facing each other across the Staffordshire platter on the writing table.

The exotic room *(right)*, with its ogee arches—repeated in the curtain treatments—its white-painted Gothic cornice, and its faint traces of chinoiserie in the pagoda-like overmantel molding, is another room in the beautiful Cornish St. Michael's Mount. (Observe how the wall color is continued on the ceiling.)

Deep blue ultramarine wallpaper and matching curtains, both covered with gilt stars, give a discreet distinction to this formal embassy salon in Istanbul. The toning blue and cream damask, used for all upholstery on the circle of nineteenth-century French seating, was very much an eighteenth-century style of decoration, with the idea that the same colors and patterns used throughout a room promoted harmony and a nice sense of cohesion. It certainly does make for a peaceful feeling, gently enlivened by the extra gilt on the frame and sconces.

Blue and white pottery, however humble, lends itself to still lifes in a quite spectacular way. Ever since the first shipment of blue and white Chinese porcelain reached the West in any quantity in the seventeenth century, it has not only been prized and collected, but copied in a myriad of different ways. Delft, the Dutch tin glaze earthenware decorated with cobalt overglaze (the same color used by the Chinese), was first, followed by the various potteries around Staffordshire in England. In the mid-eighteenth century, English potters in Bow and Worcester adopted the process of transfer printing blue images onto white pottery. This made blue and white pottery cheap enough for most people to buy, since the process was so much quicker than laborious painting by hand. Although potters originally imitated Chinese motifs, such as blossoms, pagodas, willow trees, and bridges, they rapidly moved onto pastoral settings, castles, landscapes, and, later in the nineteenth century, all-over florals. This still life in a cottage on Martha's Vineyard shows just such floral motifs with white slipware, mixed with the glass base of an oil lamp and candles. The rigging of a ship forms the background.

Dark sapphire blue could be a difficult color in flat paint, unrelieved as it is by the depth and translucence of the jewel itself. But in the narrow London room *(left),* designed by Conrad Jameson, it is cleverly contrasted with soft, pale blues and white, anchored by a dark but soft amethyst floor, and sparked by the bright violet stripe of the throw on the sofa. In the end, the whole room takes on a jewel-like feeling. The cool Majorcan room *(above),* belonging to Paco Munez, is the very opposite of the warm, jeweled tone of the former room. By repeating the blues of the sky and the sea (seen outside the long window) in the rug and pillows, the view becomes an easy extension of the room, while the yellow accents are as cooling as lemon sherbet on a hot blue day. Not everyone can have such a perfect summer view, but even without it, the blues and yellows against all the white would still look a quite stunning combination.

Any room by Stephen Sills, one of the most innovative and interesting of the new wave of American designers, is bound to be intriguing. His designs are invariably a mixture of the classical and the modern, the formal and the casual, the esoteric, the eclectic, and the familiar; but the familiar with a twist. And so it is with this graceful blue and white salon (one could hardly call it a living room), with its arcane but covetable mixture of objects. For example, there is the signed Louis XVI table by Canobas bearing its casual mix of blue flowers and eighteenth-century marble figures from England, an ancient Greek head, Roman glass, and a Charles X obelisk. Also, there are the elegant eighteenth-century English chairs covered in blue, a Mughal silver table with a skinny bronze Neoclassical urn made into a lamp, a Roman torso on its fluted pedestal, and a cube of blue mirror glass. One might expect marble walls or, at the least, a particularly exotic *faux* finish, when, in fact, the walls are full of gathered, crumpled sheets—a very *dégagé* treatment.

An intricate assembly of Bristol glass pots (named after the blue glass made in Bristol, England, during the eighteenth and nineteenth centuries), and other glass objects and boxes, make an interesting still life in the Los Angeles home of decorator Jarrett Hedborg *(left)*. But this is only part of a build-up of interesting shapes and colors in the room, from the asymmetric diamond-shaped tiles surrounding the fireplace, to the fifties molded plywood chair and tile-topped bamboo table with their vivid mauvey-blues; not to mention the stuffed blue marlin mounted in a menacing manner above the mantelpiece. The pale green background of the stenciled walls painted by Nancy Kintisch is an unusual foil for blues. Much the same coloring, but a totally different feeling, is achieved in the double-height modern room *(below)*, brilliantly scooped out of a pair of early nineteenth-century London terrace houses by the distinguished British architect Richard Rogers. The sapphire-painted structural column, the edging to the balcony, the pale blue stairs, and the blocks of aquamarine stand out with the clarity of sculpture against the bleached pallor of the walls, ceiling, and whitened floorboards. Yellow is the accent color in a New York City room *(right)*, designed by the architects Hariri, with dense cobalt blue walls. Observe too the detail of the pale blue baseboards and door frames, which soften the transition from the darker walls to the white floor.

THE DINING ROOM

A room set aside just for dining can be something of a luxury these days, especially in cities where space is invariably expensively scarce. All too often you get dining–studies; dining–workrooms; dining–guest rooms; dining–halls or galleries; dining–kitchens; dining–porches, sun rooms, or conservatories; dining tables in living rooms, or living rooms with a dining alcove; or, more felicitously, dining–libraries. All of these can be made good backgrounds for dining with appropriate color schemes, furniture arrangements, good storage, interesting table settings, and subtle lighting, so the loss of a separate room is not severely missed except when serious entertaining is required.

It might also be a comfort for the dining-roomless to remember that the dining room as a separate space did not really exist, except rarely, until late in the eighteenth century, and was not properly a separate institution until a quarter of the way through the nineteenth century. Instead, tables were set up wherever seemed most useful and most appropriate at the time. Hence the number of dismountable or expandable antique refectory, round, oval, side, and card tables dating from the late seventeenth, eighteenth, and early nineteenth centuries, and the rarity of proper dining tables from that period.

Still, the comparative rarity of the dining room at this stage in our history makes such a room a rather special place. It is a luxury to be treated traditionally, of course, if one wishes, but also imaginatively, or dramatically, or whimsically, or just extremely prettily, with the clear realization that the room is meant, above all, for the enjoyment of food with one's family and friends.

Obviously, collections of blue and white plates of whatever denomination, Chinese ginger jars, jugs and teapots, pitchers and bowls from Staffordshire, and other potteries are particularly appropriate in dining rooms and dining areas. But so is blue and white, in general. Deep, dark sapphire in velvet, or other fabric, or in a painted glaze or flat paint, will make a dining room—or room also for dining—look exceptionally distinguished, especially allied with the gleam of silver and mahogany, the crispness of white damask as cloth or napkins, the sparkle of glass and candles and possibly firelight, and the glint of gilt in picture and mirror frames. In warm climates, blue and white is one of the freshest, most tranquil combinations, making one feel automatically calmer and cooler. In the country, wherever the country happens to be, blue and white toiles, blue and white stripes from wide to narrow, blue and white checks, or just blue and white solids, and again the sparkle of candles, and, when possible, firelight, is a magical combination.

Piatto decorata con cavaliere,
XVII century tableware,
Savona, Italy

Bright, cheerful blue and white striped wallpaper, a rainbow striped rug, and blue and white patterned cotton for the tablecloth, window shade, and pillows on the couch, under the pine shelves, make a lively scheme for the dining area at one end of a Long Island kitchen. The room is simply but cleverly divided by a pair of low cupboards, which also provide useful serving space — an idea well worth emulating. Observe how the varying pinks of the azaleas, hyacinths, and primulas, and the unexpected buttery yellow of the dado (both reflected in the rug), make the piercingly blue framework of the room, with its crisp white paintwork and furniture, seem almost psychedelic. The blue message in this casual dining space is repeated again and again with the various blue and white china collectibles, as well as by the day-to-day service. It can even be seen in the blue watering can used to keep the collection of plants in the freshest possible condition.

A very stylish bordered panel of soft hand-painted blue tiles, surrounding the fireplace, acts as a gentle backdrop *(left),* to the equally stylish composition of blues on the dining table in this Greenwich, Connecticut, room. Notice how the blue-rimmed or -bordered white china is offset by the checkered blue and white napkins. Hyacinth blue tablemats, on top of a pale bluebell cloth, complement a mass of grape hyacinth bulbs exploding casually from a wooden box. And a good-looking blue, pink, and white cotton used for the chair upholstery is spiced by the darker cobalt blue of the candlesticks and soup bowl. The room is an object lesson in the delicate management of tone on tone. Blues in the large painting, and blues on the pale honey-colored wood of the table, spark up an otherwise all white space *(above),* dramatically framed by the dark, skeletal beams. This is the dining room of designer John Stefanidis' country home in Somerset, England. Beloved blue and white willow pattern plates *(right),* back an assorted collection of mostly transfer patterned jugs, prettily filled with spring flowers. They are arranged in a niche framed by old pine paneling in the dining room of a Long Island farmhouse.

There is no question that this room is a pukka dining room, decorated for that purpose alone. The grandeur of the table settings, with their blue and white English Spode china, Georgian silver, and Waterford glasses, lit by the crystal chandelier and set off by dark blue cloths, is backed by the delicacy of the hand-painted, ivory-backed chinoiserie silk wallcovering, and the Gothic tracery of the Regency chairs. Observe how the delicately wrought silver chinoiserie pagodas, in the centers of both tables, echo similar pagodas depicted on the exotic walls. And also note that the deep blue of the curtain material is repeated in the vase of delphiniums, and in the velvet sleeve wrapped around the chandelier chain, this last, a nineteenth-century custom.

Wide, bright blue and white striped wallpaper *(above),* together with a blue-painted floor, provide a strong, graphic background for this London room, designed by Richard Hudson, with its Monet-inspired yellow china and capacious white-painted hutch. The skinny iron candelabra above the table makes a nice contrast with the width of the stripes, as do the folding chairs. The more formal dining room in a London basement *(left),* although it opens right onto the kitchen, can be screened by the long blue and white curtains. The decoration of the room at night, with its plain white walls and black lacquer table, depends heavily upon the lighting provided by the dimmable inset ceiling spots and the Italian blue glass fitting over the table. Together, they make the crystal candlesticks, the Waterford glass, the old nineteenth-century cut glass decanters, and the silverware give off a splendid sparkle. The blue glass of the center light makes the flowers take on a purplish glow.

A great number of Mexican blue and white ceramics, including a collection of variegated jars, are densely arranged on solid white shelves, which more or less completely line this thick-walled tropical-style dining room in Acapulco, Mexico. The thatched ceiling, red stained chairs, contrasting with the stark black table, and, most particularly, the bright blue-lined portholes are all quite whimsical touches. All of this nicely offsets the complexity and depth of the eclectic ceramic pottery and glass collection, and the ebullient green potted fern.

The blue paint on double doors, internal window frame, and frames of the simple country chairs completely update the feeling of the dining room *(above),* in this rustic house on the Greek island of Patmos. The humming sky blue and the crisp white lace tablecloth suddenly bring a whole new freshness to the room, with its stone floor and door surround and white-painted, heavy-beamed ceiling. The room, of course, would have looked totally different if the beams had been left as natural wood and the room had had no fillip of blue paint. The spikey shapes of the small dracenae in their terracotta pots on the floor; the trailing leaves of the plant set in the inset shelves; the ancient stone amphora on the wall; the soft ochery pink of the roses in their blue and white pitcher on the table all seem to stand out with an exaggerated precision against the graphic clarity of the simple blue and white. Designed by architect Chantal Scaler, it is an object lesson on the difference color can make.

One of the most beguiling things about collecting blue and white ceramics is that unless you are a perfectionist, intent on knowing precise dates, makers, specific artists, or intent on possessing the woefully expensive translucent grandeur of rare Chinese porcelains (a passion which was supposed to have brought the American-born painter James McNeill Whistler, to near bankruptcy), you are invariably delighted with the charms of any piece that appeals to you, however cracked or imperfect, or disparate, from one another. Author and designer Barbara Ohrbach's happy jumble of nineteenth-century Staffordshire transferware and Victorian blue and white florals, as well as some ubiquitous willow pattern in the collection *(left),* in her country home, is a felicitous case in point.

Given the view of sea and sky conjoining so spectacularly just outside the windows, it would be hard to decorate the room in any other way than to repeat the same sort of coloring by day. And who would want to compete with the spectacular sunset and star-filled sky that fill the windows by night? White-painted cane chairs, lace-edged overcloth over a cream and white cotton base, blue-painted cabinet, and blue and cream chair cushions and woven rug are all deliberately down-scaled, as much in deference to the view as to appropriately casual summer living. Nor would one want to clutter up the strong shapes of the room, or in any way impede the majestic sight outside the windows. But note how the brief patches of red and white striped lounging chairs outside on the balcony, the pot of orange lilies, and the dish of strawberries all add spark to the cool of the interior of this cottage on Martha's Vineyard.

The curved blue and white walls of the striking contemporary Dutch dining room *(top left),* designed by Boris Sipek have come a long way from the homely blue and white Delft-tiled fireplaces and walls hung with Delft plates of early Netherlands interiors. The screen, placed just so as a room divider *(bottom left),* the perspective painting on the right wall, and the round reflective glass topped table, flanked by such precisely positioned chairs, is all part of a graphic blue and white composition in the dining area of this carefully arranged and uncompromisingly modern space in Houston, belonging to author Roger Kennedy. The Arts and Crafts cum Prairie School inspired decoration of the dining space *(far left)* shows how much can be made of a hall–lobby area. The soft but bright blue napkins reflect the tiny pieces of blue-stained glass in the windows, hung as striking wall decoration in the otherwise completely white space. Note the interesting contrast of the chunky table with the etiolated spare lines of the steel chairs, which are framed by the pair of long French doors.

The lightness and airiness of this nineteenth-century Swedish room are deliberately exaggerated by its blue and white scheme and the insubstantial white voile curtains, which flutter gracefully with the slightest breeze. A textured and patterned blue fabric edged with blue braid is used both as a wallcovering and as seat covers on the white lacquered chairs. Bleached floorboards (whitened with a white stain and then polyurethaned for maximum protection), and the gently colored sky blue and white rug, harmonize softly with the white woodwork, furniture, and snowy-white table runner. At night, the pale scheme, bereft of the diurnal golden light, is sparked and warmed, instead, by a generous number of flickering candles placed both on the table and in the handsome candelabra hanging above. Unusually, this charming house is still owned and lived in by the family who first built it.

THE KITCHEN

Depending upon how much you like to cook, how large the household is, and if there is space in the room to eat, even just at a counter, the kitchen is either still the heart of the home, or a passageway to and from the refrigerator, the dishwasher, and a quick cup of coffee. The latter situation is a pity, for there have never been such efficiently working, well-thought-out appliances, such well-accoutred cook tops and ovens, such thoughtfully-accessorized cabinets in every possible finish, or such a choice of countertop materials, sinks, faucets, and tiles.

If current kitchen appliance and cabinetry designers had their way, hardly a moment in the kitchen would be considered a chore. And if you only want to cosmeticize a room, to improve it by decoration alone, you can still find new oven and cabinet fronts and enamels to refresh old appliances, or you can simply replace old hardware on cabinets and paint the fronts and sides. If you happen to like cooking, or have to cook whether you like it or not, you can hardly make a mistake in designing a modern kitchen, so anxious are kitchen manufacturers to supply their wares in every possible useful permutation. If you do not like to cook, and do not need to, even the areas surrounding the refrigerator and the freezer need to be decorated. And, since a good kitchen is still one of the chief draws for potential house buyers, the room is always worth paying attention to, both practically and esthetically, even if only to maintain an investment.

Judging by the number of combinations of blues and whites that one comes across and sees in photographs, blue and white must be one of the most popular of all color juxtapositions for kitchens, and clearly always has been. So many old kitchens, whether in America or Europe, Australia or South Africa, India, South America, or the Orient, have blue and white tiled recesses for the old stove or fireplace back, that it seems to have been a particular tradition. I speak from experience, for I have twice uncovered Delft-tiled fireplaces from behind blocked up chimneys in both London and New York, that obviously had not seen the light of day for a generation or two. It is not in the least surprising, for the blue and white combination is cool in the face of kitchen heat, makes a good background both for food preparation and eating, and, in any case, as in so many rooms, makes a very pleasant juxtaposition.

In any event, blue and white for kitchens is still a popular choice. Blue and white cabinetry is in strong demand. Dark blue appliances are readily available along with dark blue enameled cookware. Large numbers of kitchens all over the world stay faithful to blue and white tiles for splash backs and behind countertop runs, for work tops themselves, and sometimes for whole walls. There is a huge choice of scrubbable blue and white patterned vinyl papers, as well as fabrics and paint shades. And, of course, there are always blue and white canisters or storage jars, dish towels, tablecloths, tableware, and old china and earthenware for decoration.

A large and ornamental slab of pale blue and white tiles covers most of the old chimney breast in this London kitchen *(left)*. It leaves just enough uncovered chimney space for a comfortable, sensibly raised fireplace, and the possibility for wood-grilling, with extra storage space for pots, pans, and other kitchen impedimenta below. The old and unusually high mantelshelf is attractively edged in similarly patterned, but much smaller scale, tiles. And it supports a collection of old continental blue and white jugs, tureens, and Brittany pottery bowls. More of the collection is stashed on the shelves of the pine hutch, or dresser, wedged into the alcove next door. In a Spanish kitchen *(above)*, another kitchen hutch also supports an extensive collection of old willow pattern, Staffordshire, and nineteenth-century scenic blue-and-white transfer design platters, as well as more day-to-day kitchenware. The collection, allied with the faded blue and white tablecloth, makes the room look very cool, fresh and inviting.

Bright cobalt blue and white walls in this efficient-looking Long Island kitchen soften the somewhat business-like air of the room with its two separate cook tops and double ovens, allowing two people to cook at the same time (or one person to prepare food for a great many people). The bright blue also peps up the monotone of the spare, wood-topped and -backed kitchen cabinets. Much the same blue is repeated in the finish of the sink, in the blue enamel saucepans and kettle, and in the abstract painting on the wall, as well as in the carefully color-coordinated wall telephone.

A small area of wall painted a warm hyacinth blue provides an esthetic counterpoint, together with the striped rug, to an otherwise mainly white Norwegian room *(left)*. Square white tiles surrounding a cook top (not quite seen under the hood) repeat the much larger panels of the door. The grayed old wood of the chairs harmonizes gently with the floorboards and grayish chimney bricks. The white boarded ceiling *(right),* and neat white woodwork and painted furniture, freshen up the old floorboards and deep blue-gray walls of this spacious and relaxing Maine kitchen–dining room, where sitting seems more the order of the day than cooking.

The original old mantelshelf has been preserved in this old French kitchen to form an interesting tonal contrast to the large area of blue and white tiles. These tiles span the former chimney breast and run under the window areas, as well as provide a useful display shelf. The double sinks sunk into the wide tiled countertop have been placed far enough apart to provide plenty of work space in between. This is a rarity in most kitchens. Brass faucets provide another nice contrast to the tiles.

Painted blue and white birds flock charmingly around the ceramic plaque above the tile-edged arch dividing the kitchen and dining areas in this Mexican kitchen *(left)*. The color of the tiles is picked up in the sloping ceiling, as well as in the painted shelves and the plain tiled edging around the sink. It can also be seen in the somewhat *dégagé* striped curtains, the canisters, and the table base.

Blue, one might say, lies in the details. The former bread oven and fireplace in the Patmos kitchen of the architect Chantal Scaler *(above),* have been recycled to house a simple stove and extra storage. Pale blue walls contrast appealingly with the old stone surrounds and deeper blue-painted oven front, and combine with the white appliances and furniture to make the ancient space look unexpectedly fresh.

A cobalt blue enameled stove and a blue tiled border stand out as bright strokes of color in an otherwise white and natural wood Australian kitchen. Note how the warm honey tones of the wood provide a pleasant mid-tone between the two basic colors. Also note how the aluminum saucepans and kettle, and the pitcher of parsley, seem particularly graphic and etched.

Deep cobalt walls give a rather dressed-up air to the relaxed Norwegian kitchen–dining–living room *(below)*, belonging to architect Rannveig Getz, as, of course, does the ornately framed late nineteenth-century mirror. Only the white tiled counter bases, and the neatly arranged shelves, give an inkling of the kitchen work areas concealed behind the tiles and sunk within. The bleached floorboards provide a gentle counterbalance to the strong blues, bright whites, and patches of black in the sofa, cooker hood, and chairs. The movie designer Richard Sherman used deliberately aged turquoise paintwork on the old breakfront kitchen units of his Hollywood kitchen *(right)*. They, along with the black-painted early Victorian furniture, brass candelabra, and wall sconces, are in striking contrast to the crisp white paint, modern recessed downlights, and the strongly geometric floor tiles, placed on the diagonal.

Note how the unexpected blue-painted stripes around the tabletop and the breakfront, the random woven cotton rugs, and the reddish-colored wood on the countertop and floor add a certain warmth and solidity to this otherwise all white Massachusetts room, designed by Estelle Guralnick. Observe, too, how a coat of white paint and dark blue stenciled flowers gives bulky, and somewhat eccentric, old turn-of-the-century furniture a great deal more appeal than it would otherwise have had. The Art Nouveau-ish motifs stenciled on the panels of the breakfront add a nice sense of whimsy. This, together with the blue-painted backs to the shelves, the blue stripe, and the blue handles turns another fairly ordinary piece of kitchen furniture into a really quite handsome-looking cabinet.

THE BED ROOM

The first priority for any bedroom should be comfort, however multifunctional its use. This is not just a question of making sure you have a mattress that is supportive, pillows that relax the neck muscles, and pleasantly soft bed linen, though all these are certainly important, given the fact that we spend a third of our lives in bed—or are supposed to.

Comfortable and well-placed lighting; comfortably capacious storage; comfortably large bedside tables to hold and, if possible, hide all the clutter; comfortable control of unwanted early morning daylight; and an easily controllable temperature are all strong factors in bedroom design. In short, like the living room, the whole ambience of a bedroom should be as comfortable, comforting, and calming as possible, which means choosing colors, textures, patterns, and furnishings that one finds relaxing and soothing to live with. Bedrooms are not rooms for drama; they should be essentially personal rooms, rooms to escape to, reconstituting rooms.

The designing of guest bedrooms is not very different. The same strictures about comfort and color choice apply. But accessories, perhaps, should not be so much personal as interesting, with every attention paid to visitors' possible needs, like water carafes, glasses, and mineral water in coolers, the odd tin of cookies, books and magazines, towels, bathrobes, and plenty of hangers, and spare toiletries, such as toothbrush, toothpaste, razors, shaving soap, and so on, for forgetful friends.

Children's rooms, in the balmy period before they start taking a hand in the design themselves, should be designed to be peaceful at first, and, if they are playrooms, too, more stimulating later. Basically, this means starting off with white, or a pastel, and adding more color in furnishings and accessories as they are needed.

Variations on blue and white are particularly appropriate for every sort of bedroom. Masculine rooms look as good in bright, medium, or dark blues, blue-background geometric, and white with different blues, as feminine rooms look with traditional paler, softer shades. Blue and white, in any shade and any pattern, design, and texture, is as safe a mid-ground for couples as it is charming and welcoming for guest rooms. Similarly, white backgrounds and soft furnishings with varying blue designs and a crisp white bedcovering create a fresh and calming ambience for both. Blue and white is not just the province for little boys, many girls are just as happy with blue. And blues and whites will happily span the years from infancy to teenager.

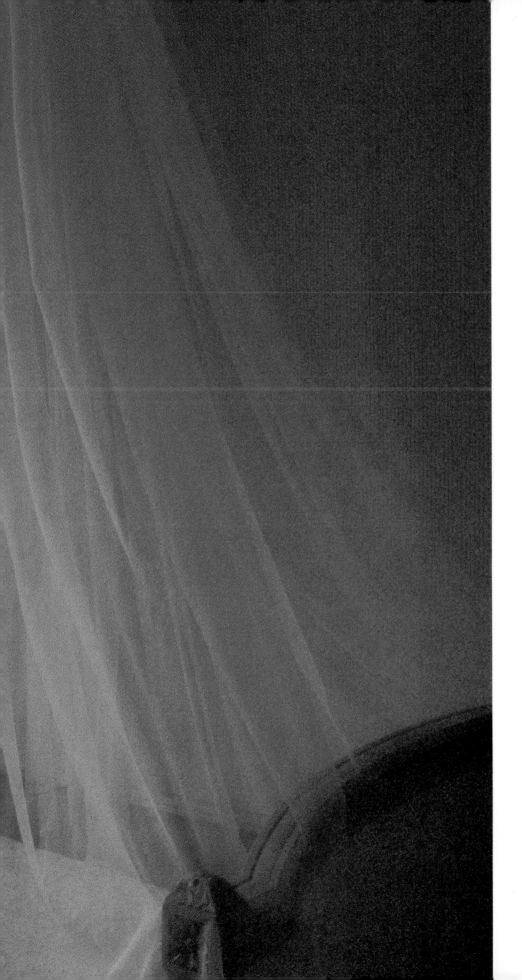

There is something wildly romantic about mosquito-netted beds, with all the connotations of life in the tropics, long siestas, scented nights, and sickle moons (even though one is almost always aware that hot, sticky nights under the nets, without any benefit from air-conditioning, is generally very far from romantic). Still, this room in the west of France, near Nantes (where they do not seem to have heard of the simple expedient of window screens) certainly does look coolly romantic. Its misty bed and shades of different blues for the walls, dado, chair, bed, and window frames are all nicely rooted by the sandalwood color of the polished floorboards and the long, blue-green view outside the casement windows.

Rich, inky blue paint in the tiny cabin on a houseboat on the River Thames belonging to Juliette Mole *(above)* makes an excellent background for a collection of black and white photographs surrounded by another collection of hats. Since the bed is placed just under the window, short curtains do double duty as part of the bed decoration, along with the tumble of white pillows piled on the blue-edged bedspread. In a quite different sort of space, graceful lengths of striped cotton are caught in a *couronne* above the middle of the bed, and then draped and twisted nonchalantly around the bedposts. This glamorous London bedroom *(right)* was designed by Mimmi O'Connell. The stripes are in graphic contrast to the soft stenciling on the walls by Peter Farlow and the ordered heap of pliable white lace pillows.

The deeply beamed ceiling in a Greek island country bedroom has been successfully softened with the prevailing blues. Forget-me-not walls, bluebell-painted woodwork, a bright cobalt blue glass light fitting, the pale hyacinth ribbon trim on the traditional local bed canopy, and the gray-blue stripes crossing the pillows on the daybed make even the white bed linens look tinged with blue. They look as if they have been washed with the old blue bag (formerly used for whitening) in the water. Since the sky outside the windows is almost always filled with the southern sun, the general daytime effect is deeply peaceful and restful.

The bleached wood bedposts making up this chunky-looking contemporary American four-poster (*above*) are much the same ivory tone as the floor, walls, and background of the rug. This makes a mellow contrast to the crisper whites and two-toned blues of the bedclothes and Roman shade, and the blue and white stripes of the bed curtains and pillow on the sofa. If the walls had been as white as the curtains and upholstery, the effect would have been sharper, less mellow. The soft tones of blue and white, for the more traditionally romantic four-poster (*left*), create an even more mellow mood, and in a grander vein. This is mostly due to the more elaborate treatment of the bed and windows, the softer designs of the fabrics, as opposed to the solid stripes of the bed above, and the elegant collection of nineteenth-century furniture.

Elaborate, and very often be-plumed, four-poster beds were very much a product of grand seventeenth- and early eighteenth-century bedrooms, which were used in equal parts for receiving visitors by day and private relaxation by night. This French bed (*right*) is an ingenious approximation of the more elaborate and substantial early versions, but made entirely from gently-patterned blue and white fabric, contrast-lined with blue and suspended from a slim brass frame. This frame, in turn, supports the canopy, topped, as can be seen, with four magnificent dark blue dyed ostrich plumes. Window curtains are treated in exactly the same way, but without the crowning feathers, and the scumbled blue and white painted wall and ceiling finish keeps to much the same tones, and has much the same effect, as the fabrics. Altogether, the room, with its lofty ceiling and old terracotta tiled floor, is a good and much more practical version of a formal early eighteenth-century bedroom, achieved at a fraction of the price.

The sturdily handsome, dark mahogany Victorian daybed in this Uruguayan bedroom–library (which is as good a mix of functions as dining room–libraries) is nicely offset by the warm bright blue of the curtains and matching bedclothes. The blue also serves to subtly soften the somewhat severe lines of the bed, floor-to-ceiling ivory bookshelves, and the long French doors. People who still profess their doubts about blue being anything other than cool, should be swayed from their opinion by the invariable effect of the color when mixed with dark, rich woods, not to mention a degree of comfortable clutter. This room is in the home of Argentine artist Nicolas Uriburu.

Dark sapphire and cornflower blue bedspreads *(above)*, along with the light fixtures, give an unexpectedly fifties air to this spacious beamed and tiled bedroom, in an old house in Patmos. To balance the powerful color blocks of the beds, the deeply-recessed window embrasures are painted the same dark sapphire, as is the frame of the sofa with its blue and white striped pillows. Much the same deep sapphire is used to paint the shutters, muntins, and frames of the windows in a Cadaqués, Northern Spain, room *(right)*. The color gently contrasts with the pale hydrangea blue walls, shutters, and bedcover, while the cobalt tiled floor is well matched with the restored painted cornice and stenciled border below. The varying blues provide a charmingly soft background for the elaboration of the late nineteenth-century bedroom suite and the chaste *broderie Anglaise* bedspread, which appears as a cool oasis of white.

The daybed *(below)*, designed by Mimmi O'Connell seems a riot of exotica, with its densely patterned tight mattress cover, the variety of designs on the comfortable cluster of pillows, the striped throw on the chair, and the prettily designed bed and window curtains, edged and contrast-lined with blue and white checkered cotton. The whole, balanced as it is on the strongly striped rug, is an object lesson in pattern mixing.

A wonderfully high canopy bed *(left)*, in a guest pavilion in Barbados, originally designed by Oliver Messel, aptly balances the soaring Palladian window which opens onto a wide terrace. The undoubted grandeur of the space is equally well counterbalanced by the simple blue and white scheme, which, if not exactly cutting the room down to size, does add a feeling of relaxation. A very different kind of bedroom *(above)*, in Devon, England, makes massive use of blue and white ribbon design cotton for upholstery, tablecloth, and looped back curtains. Only the bed is left comparatively tailored with the duvet cover outlined in blue.

Blue and white has always been a good choice for children's rooms, given the fact that most children need a calming background throughout infancy. This can be livened up with other primary colors to provide stimulation as they grow older. The pale cornflower walls certainly provide a peaceful base for the white-painted furniture, the airy blue and white checkered voile curtains, and the collection of toys (notice how the Moses basket has been recycled to hold playthings). And, just as certainly, the same blue could later absorb a variety of colored drawings, posters, prints, and the general impedimenta of growing children. The creamy floor gives the basic blue and white of the room a pleasing solidity.

The gently patterned room *(left),* in a Southampton, Long Island, show house is a great many first-time parents' dream for an infant's room, with all the romantic accoutrements of the flowing lace-draped crib, the gossamer shawl, and the charming painted furniture. The difference in this room is the remarkable effect caused by matching the wall and window coverings with the same design on the floor, giving a quite surreal effect, a softening of parameters.

The wide-striped paper on the angled roof line of this attic room in Connecticut *(right),* is the absolute antithesis of the deliberately romantic, and somewhat disorientating, room on the left. The mattress is an integral part of the shallow platform, built to make maximum use of the available space. And the geometric design of the vinyl floor underscores the crisp, clean lines and colors of a room clearly designed with ease of maintenance in mind.

A small girl's bedroom *(bottom right),* is already leaning toward the future, with twin beds ready for future sleepovers, or another sibling. Notice how the antique daybed is especially high-sided to guard against possible nocturnal excursions. Pink and blue patterned balloon shades and pillows, and pink bed skirts, compromise between traditional boy and girl color schemes.

Blue and white paint used for the walls, ceiling, floor, woodwork, iron bedstead, and night table make the most of a charming, light-filled attic space. Within this calm framework, other colors, patterns, flowers, and books stand out with a three-dimensional intensity. Windows are left unadorned to show off their shapes, to let in a maximum of light, and to act as decoration in their own right.

Grape hyacinth blue, with a bold geometric border, has been used to vastly improve what could have been a rather cramped and awkward space at the end of a New England attic bedroom. As it is, the space, entirely filled with the bed-cum-couch, seems rather inviting. The crisp navy blue and white woven bedspread has much the same feeling as the border halfway up the wall, and looks like a good place to lounge with its group of variegated pillows. Notice how the introduction of red in the tartan, the throw, and the chair and rug gives a definite fillip to these particular shades of blue.

THE BATH ROOM

One of the most comforting factors about current day bathroom decoration is that, although it is perfectly possible to spend a fortune on the most extravagant tubs, basins, showers, tiles, marble or slate, faucets (which can cost as much as a tub), and capacious storage to achieve a room with much more character, it is equally possible to expand with almost nothing at all, except time, imagination, and elbow grease. Bathrooms lend themselves to dramatic cosmetic treatment, and old bathtubs, basins, and toilets can almost always be resurfaced quite successfully, particularly if tubs are cast iron.

At best (pocket-wise), shabby or ill-conceived tiles can be painted over with gloss paint as long as their surface is roughed a little first. At worst, they can be removed and replaced, and sometimes, if there is room, retiled over the top. Scrubbable vinyl wallpapers, which come in a wide range of colors and designs, will cover over a multitude of sins—but not damp damage, which must be seen to and the cause eradicated. So, of course, can unsightly pipes below an old wall-mounted basin be disguised by a fabric skirt. Battered faucets, unsightly hardware, and cracked mirrors on cabinets can be replaced, and color in towels and a variety of accessories will make an enormous difference.

Whether the bathroom is new or old, blue and white is a natural combination for bathroom decoration. It was a favorite scheme for ancient Roman public baths, which were spectacularly and sumptuously decorated. And although it took well over nineteen hundred years for proper bathrooms with efficient plumbing and running hot and cold water to be reintroduced, as it were—a truly astounding fact, considering that cleanliness was upheld as next to Godliness—one of the first of the earliest new bathing rooms, the early nineteenth-century bathroom installed at Malmaison, for Napoleon's wife, the Empress Josephine, was also blue and white, complete with silver swans for faucets.

Now, varying shades of blue, white and blue, and white for wallpapers (if they are not vinyl, they should be first tested to see if the colors are fast, then given a coat of non-yellowing semigloss polyurethane to protect them from damp), fabrics, shades, blinds, tiles, tubs, basins, toilets, showers, faucets, towels, and, of course, blue and white floor and wall tiles, are all available to be mixed and matched in hundreds of different permutations. Walls can very well be decorated with blue-matted prints, paintings, *objets trouvés*, ceramics, plants, mirrors, and anything else one fancies, depending upon whether one looks upon the bathroom as a room for enjoyably bathing and relaxing in, or strictly as a bathing room only.

It is not very often that one can walk down a wide staircase to a spacious, elegantly windowed bathroom like this one in the Hamptons, Long Island. The centered claw-footed bath with its old faucets and hand shower, the nest of tables holding the generous vase of flowers, the lack of visible normal bathroom impedimenta, all add to the general air of graciousness. And the aquamarine shutters, the soft white-painted paneled walls, the arched top window, the louvered closet, the white of the bright white bathtub, and the painted woodwork give the room a leisurely, tropical air that is immensely appealing.

Old-fashioned, claw-footed bathtubs are now much in demand again. This one, belonging to British fashion designer Peter Sheppard, is nestled comfortably at the end of the elegantly blue-paneled bathroom *(left),* its panels gently emphasized with subtly different tones. With the blue ceiling, blue and white towels, and black lacquered oval occasional table, the room is nothing if not elegant. The addition of the well-hung art, from interestingly framed collections of old Delft tiles flanking the nineteenth-century portrait, to the collection of silhouettes above the towel rail, makes the space seem more akin to the old-fashioned, well-furbished gentleman's dressing room (alas, not much in evidence today) than to the usual bathroom.

Much of the same rather prosperous feeling exists in another gentleman's bathroom, in Hertfordshire, England, belonging to antique dealer Piers von Westenholz *(right),* where a handsome collection of traditional ivory-backed brushes and a shoehorn stand out strongly against the prevailing blue. With its thick blue carpet, intense blue-painted walls, and upscale glass-fronted shower, behind the capacious built-in closets, the room is comfortably relaxing, as well as practical for both dressing and bathing. A collection of drawings and black and white prints in simple gilt frames is well lit by the wallwasher spots, recessed into the ceiling some eighteen inches from the wall to throw an even light. The attention to lighting is also shown by the swing-arm wall lights set at either side of the mirror, which is really the best position for shaving, since the lights cast no shadows.

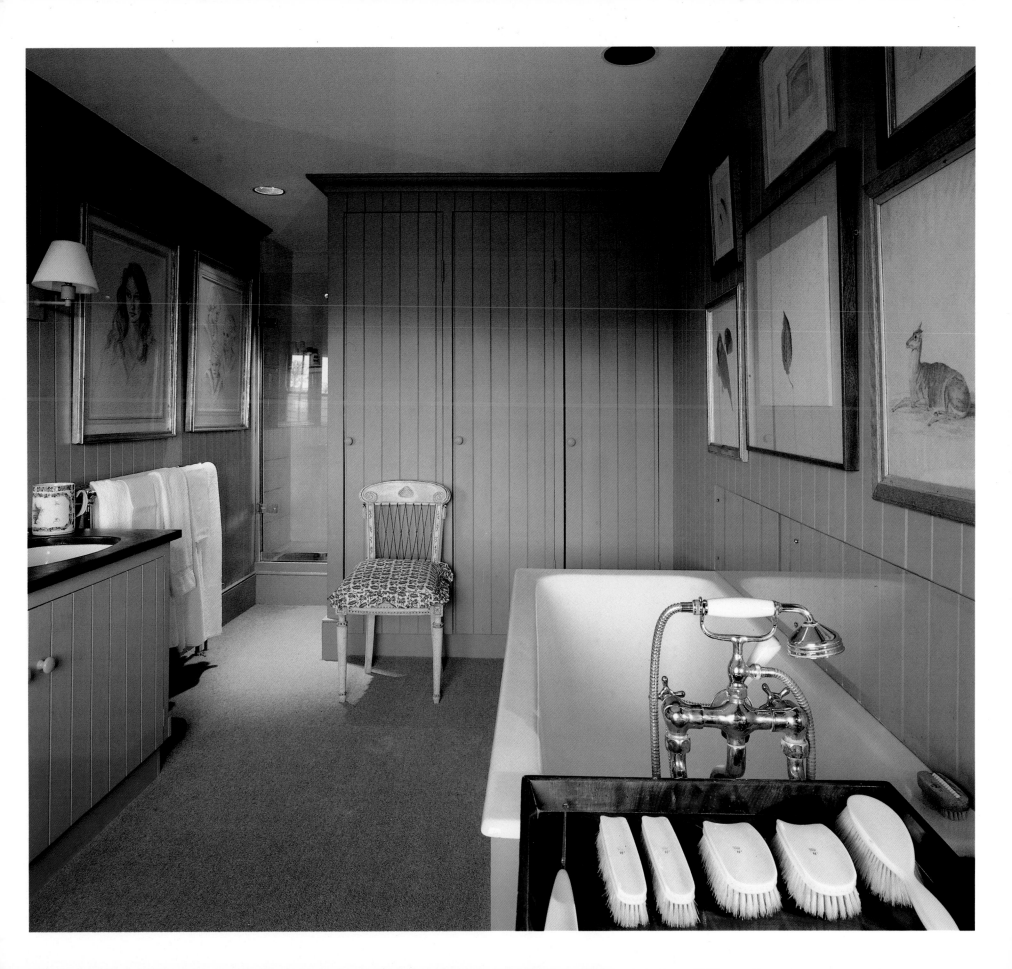

In this bright but spartan Spanish bathroom, even the window muntins are painted cornflower blue. Geometric, lozenge-shaped tiles are somewhat softened, both by their own double-edged border and by the painted ceiling trim and stenciled border above. Note the practical touches, like the separately opening grilles at the bottom of the windows and below the shutters, to allow ventilation when shutters are closed, or on *particularly* cold days. I emphasize particularly, because the room, completed in 1915, is reminiscent of the hardy 1920s, when the French doors would probably have been flung open for large and beneficial doses of thoroughly healthy fresh air. Note the wall lights around the mirror, which twist up for shaving and down for makeup. Also note a touch of finesse lacking in the circular curtain track, for what must be a somewhat claustrophobic shower, although the fittings are after all, over seventy-five years old.

An inset bathtub, with a wide, and practical, surround is the common denominator, along with the coloring, of these two widely disparate rooms. The Italian couturier Gianni Versace has a jacuzzi tub set into azure blue tiles *(left)*, in his splendid Renaissance villa overlooking Lake Como. The square-framed grisaille rondel, the panels outlined in blue, and the ornate painted and gilded cornice, not to mention the marble statuary perched on the sides of the tub, are not your everyday bathroom decoration. But they must make bathing as esthetic an experience as in the days of ancient Rome and the splendid public baths.

Bathtubs and bay windows are not often thought of in the same context, but once one sees one neatly tucked inside a surround of blue and white tiles, as in this Uruguayan room belonging to artist Nicolas Uriburu, it seems the most sybaritically obvious position—as long as one has a convenient bay window in the bathroom. It is even more special if there happens to be a long, blue view of the ocean outside.

The bathroom made out of this former London bedroom, with a Delft-tiled fireplace, is much more quiet and comfortable. The wide overmantel mirror suspended above the end of the tub is a gracious space-expander. The collection of early nineteenth-century Staffordshire transferware blue and white jugs and bowls on the mantelpiece, and the attractive cobalt blue and white Minton ewer and basin placed on the nineteenth-century pot cupboard neatly balance the blue and white of the fireplace tiles in this pleasant little room.

M odern bathrooms, designed and built as bathrooms from the start, are bound to have a very different perspective from rooms that have had bathroom fixtures superimposed on them, or old bathrooms that have been cosmetically updated with paint or paper and interesting accessories. The two modern bathrooms shown here are meant to be purely functional, with their decoration part of their form. The one room *(left)*, designed by Anger Kolff, takes an uncompromisingly high-tech approach, only minimally softened by the deliberate play on blues. The other room *(right)*, in Cologne, Germany, is another masterpiece of precision by Andrée Putman, with a place for everything and everything in its place. The white towels seem to take on a quite outstanding whiteness against the neat expanse of the soft lilac blue tiling, which reflects on and on through the mirrored alcove.

White tiles are intricately but firmly delineated with both a blue tile border and painted woodwork in a small Australian bathroom *(left)*, with its unusually shaped window overlooking a blue and white tiled courtyard. Observe the blue spotlights perched above the mirror and the carefully matching blue faucets. The London room by Pauline Boardman *(inset, right)*, however, is a good example of cosmetic improvement, with matching wallpaper and formal tied-back cotton curtains. Note the nice detail of the slim dark blue border superimposed on the leading edges of the curtains, and on the tie-backs. It is also used as a demarcation line between the tiles and the wallpaper. A rag-rolled blue paint finish to the walls in the pretty English room *(below)*, designed by Carole King, melds mistily with the soft blue and white-patterned tiled border, white voile curtains, and white wicker furniture and plant basket. The soft sky blue is gently contrasted with the deep green leaves, and looks decidedly countryish although it is actually in a London home.

In a room that appears more sculpture than ordinary living space, the blue tiled rectangular tub is used like a counterbalance to the various curves of the sweeping ceiling and the arch of the semicircular window. The same blue tiles on the wall serve to emphasize the graceful ceiling lines. The equally elegant curves of the Louis Seize *fauteuil* repeats, in its covering fabric, not only the blue of the tiles in a paler tone, but the color of the floor, window frame, and molding around the bathtub.

THE EXTERIOR

People who are literally perfectly at home with *interior* decorating schemes often have a hard time deciding upon colors for the exterior of a house. There is the decision about what color to paint the walls, the bulk of the house. Then there are the doors, the trim, and the window frames. Should they be the same color or contrasted? Should the contrast be sharp or subtle? All these questions seem somehow more vexing than how to decorate the bedroom, say, or the kitchen. Very often the decision is taken out of one's hands if there are neighbors to consider, or if you have an architect-designed house where the decisions were pre-taken, or if you happen to have an old and valued house with a preservation order and predetermined schemes. But it is all the other homes that are the problem, for an exterior scheme once executed is not as easy to change as an interior one, and generally is much more expensive when the cost of further days for the hired scaffolding has to be considered.

Porches and terrace houses, however, are a different matter. They are, after all, just other rooms, but outside. Thought about like that, any decorating decisions are often considerably easier to make.

Interestingly, whether ancient or modern, Western or Oriental, houses in the sun or houses in less benign climates, there always seem to have been some buildings somewhere that have favored blue and white for their exteriors. It can hardly be disputed that the combination stands out stylishly whatever the circumstances; whether shaming shabbier neighbors, or fitting colorfully in with a galaxy of Southern or Mediterranean pastels, or the gamut of the Postmodernist palette. And since most blues, like most greens, especially when they are teamed with white, seem to enhance rather than fight or clash with each other, there is really no need for any sort of ruling about what goes best with what for the greatest harmony.

These two houses, one an English Victorian villa *(left)*, the other a finely detailed German terrace house *(right)*, have both taken well to similar shades of periwinkle blue and white, without losing a shred of dignity. In fact, particularly in the case of the attractive German house, the wealth of unusual architectural details—the asymmetrically-placed bow window, the varying window surrounds and moldings, the finely wrought white painted muntins—have actually been exaggerated.

The soaring Northern Spanish façade *(right)*, recently restored with new tiles to match the originals, is typical of many buildings in southern Europe. It shows a somewhat Moorish influence, with its complicated molded plaster configurations around disparately shaped but symmetrically dispersed windows. The soft, cornflower blue painted moldings, muntins, and tiles, picked out as contrast to the white plaster, make an indelibly graphic impression when seen against a blazing darker blue sky. Such painted buildings are as endemic to sun-soaked areas as hot white dust, scurrying lizards, and long, lazy afternoon siestas.

A striking, wild violet blue has been used to paint the curved walls of a modern Norwegian villa *(left)*. It looks particularly good in the spring, when the color contrasts with the deep mauve of the lilac tree, and the soft white alyssum growing to the sides of the steps.

The interesting façade of the Arquitectonica Florida building *(left)*, makes great play with cobalt blue tiles and cobalt mosaic set inside, around, and below the windows, as well as above the garage doors, to make a decorative lintel. The asymmetrically placed, blue-painted window box adds a nice touch of deliberate haphazardness, as do the bright yellow flowers set against the careful composition of blue and white, framed, equally carefully, by the trees and hedge.

Dark blue painted shutters *(right)*, set on either side of a window, inset with a diamond-shaped central pane, add interest to this window on a German house. Note how the matching blue fascia boards above the window and the window box work together with the softening growths of ivy and the tangling felicitously toning climbing plant: the ever-popular clematis, Nellie Moser.

The beautifully sculptured white Majorcan villa *(left),* belonging to Paco Muniz, with its cantilevered stairway rising to a wide, shaded balcony, seems to encapsulate the sun-baked sleepy feeling of high noon all around it. The house is deliberately rooted in blue, with its lavish use of cerulean blue tiles for its spacious surrounding terrace and shallow, white-edged steps. Notice how the inset pool creates a shining rectangle in the middle of the sun-dappled blue expanse. And how the surrounding hills and trees (including the pair so carefully entrapped within the structure itself) are used to provide as green a contrast as they are able to the palpably shimmering composition of pristine white and blue. The whole *mise-en-scène* is a spectacular modern rendition of a classical Mediterranean villa, as enticing an oasis in the high dry heat as it is possible to build. In an entirely different vein, an entirely different vernacular, on the entirely different Spanish island of Ibiza, is the ancient white stucco façade *(above),* of a shaded village house. The composition of the blue door, jade letter box, battered white plaster, the freshness of deep green leaves, and the fragility of the hanging plant is pleasingly graphic.

The building *(left)*, is nothing if not true blue, right through to its reeded hyacinth blue glass windows and rickety drainpipes. Although it is clearly a poor building, in a city, Bombay, that is full of such buildings, every effort has been made to brighten it up. Note how a third, mid-toned blue has been used to outline the pipes and a slight break in the structure, where one floor very slightly overhangs the next. The elegantly converted water tower, on the River Thames in London's Docklands *(right)*, has a blue-edged, glass-sided terrace, from which to watch the floating traffic and the panorama of the city beyond. The blue and white awnings, and the blue-painted side porch, are as handsome an addition to the somber gray brick as are the gracefully arched windows, with their pale stone quoins and unexpected circular muntins. The frailty of the spiral staircase seen against the bulk of the tower-like structure is also very appealing.

The possession of a high roof terrace in a city, in this case Los Angeles, can be like going upstairs for a vacation. There, one is lazing nonchalantly above, and the city teems beneath. The contrast, whether basking lazily in the hot, high blue of midday, or sipping cold wine in the warmth of a grapey-dusk, is almost an elixir in itself. Here, the illusion of a separate life aloft is further aided by the pale bluebell tiled floor, which turns into sapphire in the shadow, the white-painted Adirondack chairs, sloped back for easier relaxation, and the terracotta pots, with all their Mediterranean associations. Tips of cypresses and palm tree fronds peeking over the roofline are also evocations of an island hideaway.

High tech–low tech: The common denominator of both of these spaces, so opposite to each other in feeling, is the cool of the blues against the ravages of summer heat and light. The Lego-like balcony *(left)*, in Australia, boasts an interesting combination of turquoise for the chairs, mixed with mid-blue and white, set high over the green of the trees below, which looks cool on the hottest of days. The balcony is also somewhat sheltered by the raftered roof above and the pierced blue metalwork, which filters the sun. The shadier porch *(above)*, in Sweden, the home of the architect Peter Celsing, also combines blue walls and upholstery with turquoise as the ceiling color. But the shiny pale bleached floor, casual white-painted furniture, and French doors are leavened as much by the unexpected formality of the blond Louis XVI style chairs as by the sandalwood color of all the chair cushions and the green pillows on the sofa.

Just a touch of blue, as in the trio of propped cobalt painted ladders *(left)*, against a Maine building, is apt to focus the eye more sharply onto an otherwise all-white mass. And certainly, in this case, the extra attention would be worth it. The combination of textures on the façade of the building and its neighbor is quite charming, with the mixture of clapboard and stripes of rounded shingles. An equally charming old Maine house *(right)*, a relic nobody had the heart to relinquish when the modern industrial buildings went up all around, has not only a splendidly curving and highly decorative balcony, but it is also splendidly blue. It is blue from the painted clapboarding to the balustrade and trellis, all jauntily spiced with the white of the pillars and decorative ironwork. Although this landmark house looks so domesticated, it has actually been converted inside for office and commercial use.

Swimming pools sunk right next to the ocean, as this one in Majorca, seem to me, at least, somewhat surreal, as if they are improving on nature in rather too familiar a way. In any case, they are certainly taming it. No waves need hinder the obligatory daily lengths; no sand gets inside bathing suits or hair. One can even have fresh water rather than salt. What you do get, of course, is an exaggerated sense of space, and air, and an enveloping blueness. This is exaggerated even further by the surrounding sky blue tiles, and the still reflective water, which seems to have captured and held the echoing blue of the sky. Only the surrounding white-painted wall seems to hold back the vastness of the sea.

Photography Credits